THE POWER OF
PURPOSE IN LIFE

SUCCESS STORIES OF ORDINARY PEOPLE
WITH EXTRA ORDINARY DREAMS

KRISHNA GANESH

BALBOA.
PRESS

A DIVISION OF HAY HOUSE

Balboa Press books may be ordered through booksellers or by contacting:

Balboa Press
A Division of Hay House
1663 Liberty Drive
Bloomington, IN 47403
www.balboapress.com
1-(877) 407-4847

ISBN: 978-1-4525-6687-0 (sc)
ISBN: 978-1-4525-6688-7 (e)

Printed in the United States of America

Balboa Press rev. date: 04/23/2013

DEDICATION

This book is dedicated to my beloved parents, Mr. Kalmanje Raghupathy Acharya and Mrs. Sukanya Raghupathy Acharya. They raised me up with all the affection and care, teaching my siblings and me all the virtues and the values that made me what I am today, and I really thank them from the deepest of my heart for that.

I am very happy to bring out this book on the auspicious occasion of my dear father's seventieth birthday. I thank the almighty for blessing them with a long and happy life.

CONTENTS

ACKNOWLEDGMENTS

I would like to thank my beloved wife, Veena, for all her support in writing this book. I do not know if I could have written this book without her constant encouragement, especially when I seem to be in the slow and indolence mode. She has been my beacon and the wind beneath my wings throughout my life. I thank my loving children, Master Vittal and Miss Srilakshmi, for their support and cooperation.

I thank my in-laws, Mrs. Sneha Tantry and Mr. B. Ramdas Tantry, for encouraging me to write this book, and special thanks to my father-in-law for proofreading my manuscript.

I thank my sister, Roopa, and her husband, Mr. Shivaprakash; my brother, Mr. Santhosh Kumar Raghupathy, and his wife, Dr. Chetana; and also my brother-in-law, Mr. Prasad Tantry, and his wife, Ramya, for all of their encouragement over the years. They have been pillars of support for me, especially when I lost my two-and-half-year-old beloved child, Srinidhi.

I also thank Mr. Muralidhara Rao for helping me in writing the success story of Mr. P. Ramadas, who is an industrialist and a trendsetter in building a highly successful business venture in the much-acclaimed, knowledge-based manufacturing sector in India.

I would also like to thank my guru, Shri Bannanje Govindacharya, for teaching me the art of soul-searching in life. His advice to do serious introspection on God, the nature, and my life has gotten me answers for some of my difficult questions about life. This later became the inspiration for writing this book.

I would like to thank Mr. Anupam Acharya for prompting me to write this book. Also, I would like to thank the Balboa team, the publishers of this book, for their support in bringing it out professionally and on time. Last but not least, I would like to thank all those who have directly or indirectly helped me in writing this book.

FOREWORD

There is a saying: if life exists, then it is the purpose that counts. At a time when the world is ridden with strife due to radicalization of the religions, atrocities, domestic violence, and the struggle due to unemployment, the timing of launching this book, *The Power of Purpose in Life*, seems perfect.

Life needs a purpose so that one can reach a higher level of existence. Various studies and researchers have concluded that the lack of purpose or aim in people's lives is one of the fundamental reasons behind all the negativity in society. The deficiency of aim in life makes people wander and waste their precious time doing no constructive work. People with no purpose in life seem to just wander aimlessly and idle around letting their idle minds turn into the devil's workshop. No noble thoughts can ever come into such negative minds. In a nutshell, this negative mood is the seed or the root cause for most of people's misery. If society ever needed people who can motivate others to have some purpose in life, it is now.

On a day when we are bursting with happiness, have we asked the question, "What is the purpose of life?" We haven't. That is, in fact, a question we ask ourselves only when life gets a little sedate and depressing. One has to inspire and motivate oneself by looking at the lives of people who have left a legacy behind them.

When Mr. Krishna approached me about wanting to write a success story of my achievements in life to inspire others, I was humbled and more than happy to be a part of this great initiative. He is writing for a cause, and I am glad that I am, in a way, helping to bring about a change in society.

He has written inspiring stories about my achievements and others who made it big in life irrespective of all the problems we have in India. People generally keep blaming others or circumstances when there are failures in their lives and simply give up. They are termed as mediocre people. But those who have the intense desire to accomplish something in life will do it, no matter what the external conditions are. They are termed as achievers. Great people make things happen, while mediocre people complain about everything; that's the difference. All the heroes whose success stories have been captured by Krishna have demonstrated that their sincere hard work, perseverance and passion for what there were doing ultimately brought success in their lives.

This book really attempts to help serious readers find their natural abilities and use them to find a purpose of life. Krishna has rightly said that everyone has inherent abilities by birth. I also agree with him that all of us are talented and blessed with at least one skill, and it is this skill that can bring success to us. He explains in detail how to find this skill by way of questioning ourselves and looking for the answers within. I am sure that this will work, as most of the mysteries that mankind has ever solved have been through contemplation.

As far as my life is concerned, whatever I have achieved today is due to my determination, my dedication to hard work, a positive attitude, perseverance, and the passion to excel in life. My company, Ace Manufacturing Systems Limited (AMSL), is one of the largest machine tool builders in the country and aspires to be one among the top ten in the world by 2020. This has been our mission and purpose.

Krishna's passion is to inspire others to bring success in their lives, and with his corporate background of more than twenty years, he makes an ideal person for this. In fact, he gives motivational speeches and conducts workshops exhorting people to have some purpose in life. On the occasion of launching of this book, I wish him all the best and pray to God to bring success in his endeavor to motivate people through his book.

Mr. P. Ramadas
managing director (MD),
Ace Manufacturing Services Ltd. (AMSL)
Bangalore, India

Brief Introduction
of Krishna Ganesh

I am Krishna Ganesh from Bangalore, India. I am a successful professional with more than twenty years of corporate experience. I worked for several multinational companies (MNC) until 2010. While at work, I managed information technology (IT)–related software projects. Though I was in well-paid jobs for more than twenty years, my heart was elsewhere. I always felt hollowness, as I was not enjoying what I was doing. I was like any other person in the corporate world, working for the sake of surviving.

My life went on that way until the year 2008 when I suddenly lost my beloved two-and-half-year-old, healthy child. It was a severe blow to me. Life started appearing superficial to me. I felt like I was missing something. I set out in search of an understanding of the meaning of life and the purpose behind our existence, but my search was in vain. I was keen to know the recipe for happiness in life. In 2010, I went for a ten-day Vipassana, a Buddhist meditation retreat, in a remote village on the outskirts of Bangalore. That was when my questions were answered. During the retreat, we were not allowed to talk for ten days, and for most of the daytime, we were made to meditate.

I had a deep introspection on life while watching nature. I saw birds, butterflies, insects, and frogs at peace with themselves, and they seemed so joyful. The wild trees giving shelter to these creatures were gigantic in size. And all of them, including the trees, were looking good and well fed. This was inspite of the fact that no human was ever caring for them. The melodious chirping of birds in the early morning seemed to bring so much peace in me. These creatures haven't received an MBA or PhD in any subject. There is no career for them and no monthly income. Yet they seem to be happier living harmoniously with nature, unlike humans. Why is that so?

What May Be the Reason?

I realized that whoever has brought these living beings into this world, it is his responsibility to take care of them with shelter and food until they die.

In this case, it is God. The creatures in nature just live for the moment and never think or worry about their next meal. This kind of life keeps them happy without any anxiety, as they do not overly think about the future.

Humans are also living beings, like those mentioned above, with one exception. They have intellect and can think, unlike other creatures. God has brought humans on this planet as a grace to let them do whatever they like in life, be it becoming a singer, a dramatist, a doctor, a chef, a scientist, a philosopher, or the like. When it comes to survival of the humans, God does not differentiate humans from other animals; it is still God's responsibility to take care of them. All that one has to do in life is pursue one's passion without worrying about survivability.

To further simplify it, God's message is that one has to make an effort to excel in life in whichever area he or she has a natural ability. He (God) takes care of the rest.

When one excels, success comes along with name, fame, and money naturally. But when one constantly worries about the perceived uncertain future, one cannot give one's 100 percent and will fail. Success will evade him or her and so will name, fame, and money.

How Does One Know Which Line One Should Choose for Building One's Career?

It was at the retreat that I learnt about the survival skill or natural ability that every living being is blessed with. One has to find this

God-given ability and pursue the profession in line with one's natural skill by birth. Also, I found my natural skill. Though I did not enjoy the kind of work I did throughout my career life, I realized I had a natural knack for inspiring, motivating, coaching, and counseling people. These skills have been with me from the beginning, since birth, and not through attending any external training. It is just that I did not notice it till I made a serious self-inquiry about myself. This skill was very natural for me, and I eventually developed passion to use it to make a difference in people's lives.

My Life after the Vipassana Meditation Retreat

I quit my job in 2010 and started a venture to motivate young people through motivational speeches and workshops to bring excellence to their lives. The youngsters need a lot of motivation as they become future citizens. Their success will lead to a harmonious living in society. I have been persuading them to have hunger for something in life. Life becomes worthy once we attach a purpose to it. This has been proven time and again. All the major discoveries, explorations, inventions, innovations, etc., happened as a result of passion, purpose, hard work, and perseverance. Apart from this, one of my hobbies has been to study the lives of those people who have made it big in life. I was curious to know the reason behind their success. The result of my study of these individuals has helped me bring out this book.

What Is the Purpose of My Life?

The purpose of my life is to help people bring success to their lives. In this way, I can realize God and be content in life. I am very happy and blissful because my career is no more work but a passion of mine.

PREFACE

If there is one thing that people—irrespective of race, religion, and country—want, it is happiness; the one thing they dislike is sadness. Happiness is very subjective and is tied to many things in life. One can be happy when one becomes a father or a mother. With the arrival of an infant at home, parents will naturally be ecstatic. Similarly, one will be happy when one finds a life partner of one's choice and gets married. A businessman is happy when he receives business from his client. A singer is happy when she gets to sing for an award-winning film. Likewise, a scientist is happy when his experiments yield the desired results, and so on.

So, different people are happy for different reasons. Note, however, that the happiness these people have is temporary and not long lasting. For example, a married couple's joy of having a baby fades away as time passes and is no more as ecstatic a joy after some years. It may turn out to be a pain if their kid becomes a brat. It is true with lovers and also with everything in life.

So, What Keeps a Man Happy throughout His Life?

The answer to this question is "purpose of life." This could seem strange because, at first, there does not appear to be a connection between the two. On closer observation, a connection becomes clearer. The purpose gives an identity for everyone.

Statements such as "I am a musician," "I am a rocket scientist," "I am a businessman," "I am a photographer," "I am a singer," etc., emerge from identity. So, when the purpose of life is not defined sufficiently, it results in an identity crisis leading to low self-esteem and is one of the root causes for disenchantment with one's life. Everyone has a faint idea about one's purpose, which is derived out of one's profession. That means the profession is defining one's purpose, which is not strong enough to give happiness. Rather, the profession should be a reflection of one's purpose. A strong purpose gives a person happiness that is long lasting.

To explain in detail, millions of people work as technicians, software professionals, scientists, business executives, etc. When probed, we find that most of them are working in their respective professions as a means to make ends meet, which essentially means to survive in life. This explains why organizations, in spite of employing many scientists and innovators, still lack the punch when it comes to producing pathbreaking products. The reason could be that most scientists may be merely doing their jobs and nothing beyond that. There is no passion for what they are doing, and this shows in the result of their work. A strong purpose brings in passion, which, in turn, makes the person excel in life. However, there is a strong linkage of purpose to one's natural abilities or skills. If one finds what one's natural, God-given skill is, it is easy to find a purpose in life.

Why Is It Important to Have Purpose in Life?

Life happens to be uncertain; no one knows how long one will live. So, as long as one is healthy, one should make life worth living by engaging in some activities that are of one's liking and that use innate skills. This is important as God has given each person one life to live, and it is worth making use of it for accomplishing some goals. The goals so chosen by individuals should never destroy nature and should add value to society for harmonious living. Having lifelong goals loosely defines one's purpose of life.

Not having a purpose in life means letting one's potential rust, thus bringing misery to oneself and wasting God-given abilities. This is as bad as a bird being lazy and not flying to find its food, irrespective of the fact that it has God-given wings to fly.

This book talks in detail about the benefits of having a purpose in life. Also, an attempt is made to help serious readers find theirs using their ingrained skills. I have talked about this skill at length in this book. I have also explained with examples to prove how specific purpose can be found using these inbred skills. My intention behind writing this book is to inspire and motivate youngsters to find their purpose of life and work toward it with passion. Life seems to be so good and happening when we follow our passion. As a step in that direction, I have included real-life stories of ordinary people who made it big in life, beating all the odds. This is the result of my study and analysis of lives of such people for the past few years. These stories narrate how working with purpose and passion helped these individuals make some blockbuster products. These stories also talk about how small companies of yesteryear went on to become major multinational corporations (MNCs) within a period of a decade or two. Their stories are truly inspiring. If you want to know more about the people or the heroes of these stories, their products, and the organizations they lead, their website addresses are given below each story.

Why Are Only Success Stories of Indians Mentioned in This Book?

In spite of its big size, India ranks low, at 132 out of 183, in the 2012 World Bank global ranking survey of countries for ease of doing business. The scale starts from 1, which implies being on top in the rankings in ease of doing business; the low ranking of 132 represents difficulty of doing business. In spite of facing many hurdles to start and run their businesses, the people in my stories have really done a fantastic job in transforming their normal start-ups to global giants by 2012. So it is all the more important to tell their stories first, rather than the stories of their counterparts in the United States of America (USA), Germany, or France where the environment for doing business is very conducive.

So, if a person from India can succeed in harsh environments, people elsewhere can succeed too—in fact, with much more ease. These stories can instill hope and confidence in the readers that they too can succeed in whatever they are doing, provided they work hard with passion and a strong purpose. I encourage readers not to worry much about where these companies are based. Rather, they have to understand how these people achieved success in spite of the tough environment they were operating in. Another reason for success stories on Indians first is because I reside in India.

Please note that the revenue figures, profit margins, etc. that have been quoted in the stories may change, as they depend on many factors. Instead of focusing on these figures, readers will gain a lot if they try to understand the efforts that have gone into the making of iconic products and the companies.

Also note that the data for these stories has come from diverse places on the Internet, and writing inspiring stories using the data is purely my effort. The intention behind reporting their success stories is that, it is easier to convey the message directly to the readers this way than through bland narration.

INDIA: A BRIEF INTRODUCTION

India is a continent-sized country in South Asia. She has a population of more than one billion people, with a majority of them being young and of an average age of younger than twenty-five years old.

India has been a socialist country from the day she attained independence on August 15, 1947. Newly independent India was under the influence of the erstwhile United Soviet Socialist Republic (USSR), and because of that, it chose the socialistic way of life.

A socialist government meant control of everything that India produced, marketed, and distributed. The government's influence was everywhere. All activities—whether they be economic, political, social, or otherwise—demanded licenses, and the government was the ultimate authority on issuing, renewing, and revoking them. Since the actions of the government were not according to market dynamics, there was a lot of supply-and-demand mismatch. This resulted in scarcity-like situation in all the aspects of life.

Import duty was prohibitively high, and the government discouraged foreign direct investment (FDI). Exports were negligibly low as there was scarcity. This made the local manufacturers very arrogant, because there was no competition from technologically superior products from foreign producers. The manufacturers continued to make and sell their shoddy products to the Indian customers and made lots of money. This license saga continued till 1991 when India faced the balance of payment (BOP) crises. That means the government had no money to import essential commodities, and no one was willing to give loans to the government. India, under pressure from international banks, such as the International Monetary Fund (IMF) and the World Bank, reduced import duty and broke some of the hurdles for foreign companies to do business. That was how the economic reforms began—not willingly, though.

So, India embraced the market economy as early as 1991 when a few hurdles for doing business were removed.

MNC companies found the burgeoning Indian middle class an attractive proposition to do business with, and the idea was hard to resist. Though India has many booming cities, the key drivers of the Indian economy come from a few big cities like Mumbai, Delhi, Kolkata, Chennai, Hyderabad, Bangalore, and Pune. Out of these, Bangalore is considered to be the technology hub of South Asia. It is also ranked as the world's ninth-largest start-up hub as per the 2012 report of *Startup Genome*, a reputed start-up tracker. General Electric (GE) has the world's second-largest laboratory working on futuristic technologies in Bangalore, housing thousands of scientists; other companies located in Bangalore include Cisco, Microsoft, and Shell Petroleum. Naturally, Bangalore is the technology capital of India. Similarly, Chennai has become South Asia's auto hub with more than a million cars and heavy-duty trucks being manufactured there. A lot of automobile research also happens in the city. Mumbai is known as the financial capital, and Delhi is the political capital of India.

Indian currency is called rupees (Rs.), and it trades on an average at Rs. 50 against US$1. The exchange rate is approximated at 50, as it is easier for calculation purpose. That means in 2012, US$1 can fetch 50 Indian rupees.

In the stories, the revenues and the profits of the organizations mentioned may look very minuscule when compared to the US dollar. This is because of the fact that the Indian rupee depreciated more than 40 percent over a decade. Because of this, it has nothing to do with the companies' performance but everything to do with the Indian government's policies, which has improved in recent times.

Terminologies and Abbreviations Used

Lakh: One hundred thousand Indian rupees is one lakh.

Crore: One hundred lakh Indian rupees is a crore, which is also ten million rupees.

Hundred crore: One billion Indian rupees is one hundred crore.

USD: United States dollar.

cc: Cubic centimeters, a term used in defining the size of an automobile engine. The bigger the cc size, the more powerful the engine.

BPO: Business process outsourcing. Companies in the United States and Europe outsource their business processes to vendors who may get the processing done in countries with cheap labor like India, Philippines, Malaysia, Eastern Europe, China, etc., to reduce the cost of operations and save money.

CNC lathe: Computer numerically controlled lathe.

SPM: Special purpose machines.

IT: Information technology.

Importance of Finding the Purpose of Life

What is it like getting into a car, fully dressed, with a tank full of petrol, but not knowing where to go? This kind of journey takes passengers nowhere—it keeps them on the road, takes them through twists and turns, but eventually brings them back to where they started.

Human life can be compared to a vehicle on the move. Like a conventional car driver who has full control of the car while it is moving, one also has to have full control of one's life to direct himself toward his set of desired objectives. Like every journey begins with the knowledge of the destination to be reached, life also has to have a clear knowledge of its destination. The destination in life is nothing but what one wants to be in life: a doctor, a surgeon, an astronomer, a scientist, a biotechnologist, a businessman, a musician, or any number of other things, and, above all, a good human being.

When one's higher purpose is known and is clear, then the most crucial activities, like framing the road map or preparing a concrete plan to achieve what one aspires to be, would begin. The road map needs to be divided into short—and medium-term plans with the expected end results and the time domain. When we have a plan with clear end results and dates ready, it is like having a Google map in our hand to reach our destination. So, like our physical journey, life's journey will also be that much easier.

Though the above facts are not something unknown to people, why is that we see a majority of the people in our society struggle and wander around with no aim in life? It is partly because we have been brainwashed by everyone around us, as far back as our childhood days, to put an effort to survive in life. Surviving in life is akin to

1

walking on a tightrope with a pole in hand. There is always a risk of falling. When we are in college, all our hard work, nights out, sweating it out, are just to get good scores so that we get jobs in good companies. Our only purpose to study is for a degree certificate and good scores—nothing beyond that. It is just to learn to earn.

Once we join a company, our daily chores and struggles are only for getting good performance ratings so that we qualify for appreciation and salary hikes. We call this progress. The purpose is very shallow here, and it doesn't inspire us. When we tend to lead a pocket-to-mouth life like this, one day we suddenly realize we are redundant for the company and may be laid off. In spite of this, if we continue leading life further, we may end up becoming redundant in life too, making life very problematic and troublesome, littered with fear of failures, adversities, and pitfalls. The solution to such problems lies in finding a long-term, meaningful, and, yet, demanding purpose. It should be strong enough to inspire and engage us with the purpose passionately.

Why Is "Finding Purpose" in Life So Important?

The answer to this question is that our happiness, which is so precious, is tied to this, and our much-required self-esteem is hinged on the purpose of life. For those who have no purpose in life, there is a high probability that they will suffer from low self-esteem, which is one of the main reasons for sadness and depression and may eventually trigger suicidal thoughts.

The purpose is like a mission statement for the individual that states why that individual exists. It also states the objective behind one's being alive. This is similar to the mission statement of any company. The mission statement conveys the objective behind the starting of a company.

For example, the mission statement of Facebook says: "Facebook's mission is to give people the power to share and make the world more open and connected", (https://www.facebook.com/facebook/info). Similarly, for Google it is: "Google's mission is to organize the world's information and make it universally accessible and useful", (http://www.google.co.in/about/company/) For Microsoft, it is: "Microsoft's mission is to enable people and businesses throughout the world to realize their full potential", (http://www.microsoft.com/about/en/us/default.aspx). The higher the purpose in life, the higher is the self-esteem, resulting in higher levels of happiness and joy.

To explain in detail: Everyone knows that most people in modern societies work day in and day out from early morning to late in the night, like machines. When we ask them the reason behind it, most have either no answer or have reasons such as paying mortgages, repaying loans, or educating their kids. However, as valid as such answers may be, they should never be the only purpose for working. There has to be some higher cause—a higher goal—that motivates people. The purpose behind work should be positive enough to give them happiness.

When compared to the above case, consider someone who is working hard doing day-to-day chores but with a higher purpose. The following example can be taken for analysis.

If one's purpose in life were to become a leading scientist and experiment on future technologies, one would make sure that one's daily chores included something that leads to that goal. One would generally be joyful. This is because one is enthusiastically visualizing oneself approaching the life's goal on a day-to-day basis. This person may work as hard as or harder than others; the purpose to work, however, is not to pay back loans or educate kids but to work toward turning a dream into a reality. This hard work fetches good returns like name, fame, money, etc.; hence, it is joyful.

Also, all the perils of modern societies, such as violence due to hatred for other races, religions, etc., and domestic violence, suicides, and so on are because of the fact that people have no strong purpose in their lives. The mind is generally negative—or, to put it another way, the mind always tends to lean toward negativity. But it takes a lot of effort for one to push one's mind toward positivity. What better way than to keep the mind in positive mode by engaging or binding it with a strong purpose of life?

A strong purpose brings hope, aspirations, and the required drive to work hard in life. It also gives meaning to life. Whoever has a purpose in life has a reason to live passionately. One will never indulge in any negative activity and will generally be happy and peace loving. When a society is made up of such people, there will be peace, prosperity, respect for each other, and harmony. So it is all the more important to encourage people to find the purpose for their lives.

How Does Success Come in Life?

Success comes with hard work, passion, and strong purpose behind one's work. If the skill used in the work is natural for the individual, then success is guaranteed.

What Is Natural Skill?

God has blessed every living being on the planet Earth with one distinctive or unique skill, called a survival skill, be it animals, birds, bees, worms, reptiles, humans, and others. For example, honeybees have the natural skills to suck honey from flowers; they do it so well that they don't harm the flower but help in pollination. They also have the skill to build honeycombs with the wax that naturally comes from their bodies. They do it perfectly without any strain. It is difficult or impossible for other living beings to copy that.

Fish have the natural skill to effortlessly swim in water. Birds have the natural ability to fly without falling from the sky, unlike humans who fly in airplanes. This shows that human beings' efforts in flying are not natural but borrowed. Similarly, birds living in deep jungles build nests, lay eggs, and hatch them. When their offspring are in the nests, these birds fly for several miles every day looking for grains, worms, etc. They pick up what they want and come back to the same nests and feed their offspring. What is amazing is how they know which branch of which tree has their nests. This is difficult to trace because jungles have millions of trees, shrubs, bushes, etc.

What makes them come back home to their offspring from faraway places with clocklike precision? The answer is that God has given that unique skill to birds. But humans are deprived of this. If humans decide to do that, they will need state-of-the-art gizmos like satellite navigation systems (SNS), geographical positioning systems (GPS), walkie-talkies, etc. Even then there could be a possibility that they would arrive at the wrong destination. Why is it so? The answer is: God hasn't given this natural skill to humans. It is as simple as that.

But humans have different sets of natural skills. They are blessed with intellect and the ability to choose what they want to do in life. Apart from this, each and every individual has some kind of inborn instinctive skills, or survival skills. For example, some people have natural skills in speaking. Some have the natural ability to mingle with others, some have skills in creativity and art, and yet others can think scientifically and do best when they are in research and development (R&D) Similarly, a few people have a knack for teaching school kids or university students. Some have a knack for doing business, some others make good administrators, a few may have a flair for engineering work—the list is endless. So, whatever comes naturally or spontaneously to us are our natural skills. When these skills are used in our chosen professions, success comes to us with little effort. In contrast to this, success does come even when we work on borrowed skills, but with lots of hardship and at the cost of health.

To explain further, if a person who has a natural skill and ability in technology development is working as a salesperson for a company, he or she will undergo severe stress and frustration. No amount of exercises and positive talk can help subside the stress and exhaustion. Instead of treating the symptom, one should go to the cause of it. That is, the person should make a career change from sales to R&D; the stress and frustration will naturally turn to joy and happiness. To make this point more illustrative, let us take another example: one who has the natural skill for singing will generally have the life's purpose to become a famous singer and excel in singing. This person may not do well or may even fail sometimes if he or she takes up, for example, solving mathematic formulas as life's only purpose. This is because mathematics is not that person's natural skill but a borrowed one, unlike singing. This is why one's profession should make use of one's natural abilities. That is when success comes naturally and without major efforts. It is also joyful, because work is not merely a profession but a hobby.

When someone gets to make use of his natural skills and is generally joyful, it is still important to find a long-term purpose of life. Otherwise, the enthusiasm and joy will fizzle out after some time. This is because making a hobby one's profession may not remain so for long, unless we consciously make it so. For this to happen, the purpose plays a prominent role. In a nutshell, the person should make an effort to have some purpose in life. It could be an extension of her natural skill or ability. That is singing in the above case.

Passion and the Art of Finding Purpose in Life

One's natural abilities and passion are connected. To understand this point clearly, let us take an example. If someone working as an accountant in a company has an interest or passion for cooking food, the person's heart lies not in accounting but in cooking. It is a given that any work is done perfectly when the doer does it from the heart. So, realizing that person's big dream in the cooking domain is easier than in the accounting domain. So, to become a world-class, award-winning chef can be the purpose of that person's life, and it can be easily achieved.

The role of passion was brilliantly demonstrated in the life of Buddha, one of the greatest philosophers the world has ever seen. Before he became Buddha, he was a prince called Siddhartha who had all the luxuries of his life. Though he was a prince, his heart was elsewhere. He had a natural interest or liking for finding a lasting solution to the miseries of mankind. He renounced everything, looked for a solution, and did great penance meditating for months and skipping food and water. He did it from his heart, and hence, he succeeded in his endeavor. Introspecting on life, trying to understand and unravel the mysteries of it, was a natural, God-given gift for Siddhartha. He used it effectively to find a philosophical solution to human problems and became a star among philosophers. His purpose of life coincided with his passion.

Similarly, the late Mother Theresa rendered yeoman social service for the welfare of poor people. Her compassion for the poor and the needy was real and intense. She was always ready to help them and never tired of her work because of this. Thousands of people benefited from her, and her love for them was God-given and natural to her. She earned such name and fame from her passionate work that others could only dream of. She never underwent any training on social service, but went on to deliver world-class service to mankind. It is difficult to believe, but it is true. It happened that way because serving people was an inborn skill for her, and she used it efficiently. Had it not been her passion for her work, she would have worked just like anyone for the sake of money between nine o'clock in the morning and six o'clock in the evening with Sundays off. As a token of appreciation, she was conferred the Noble Prize for her work. Her purpose of life was to serve mankind, which gelled well with her passion.

Thomas Alva Edison, a school dropout, went on to become the world's greatest product inventor and marketer. He holds more than one thousand US patents and is partly responsible for the modern world. Marketing was his core skill, and innovation was his passion; he used them to their fullest extent to bring unprecedented success to himself. The American company GE, with more than US$150 billion in revenues, as of 2012, was founded by him. His passion and lifelong obsession with product innovation became the purpose of his life.

Similarly, Nicola Tesla, the great poster boy of invention and innovation, was also a school dropout like Edison but worked with him later to invent alternating current (AC), the AC induction motor, and other things. These have now become a part of our lives. The skills required to excel in his work came from within, as he neither attended any course nor underwent any training. It was his passion for invention and innovation that made him work hard and excel in his life. Tesla showed no great interest in marketing his products, unlike Edison, who became a great businessman in the later part of his life. Marketing was not Tesla's core skill; hence, he showed no big interest in it. This shows that people generally excel in areas they have natural abilities in. The purpose of Tesla's life was built on the foundation of his natural abilities and passion. This shows that efforts in knowing one's passion will not go to waste; they can pay rich dividends to the individual. There is a strong connection between one's passion and inherent abilities.

How Is This Passion Connected to the Natural Skill?

Generally, passion and natural skills are connected. For example, if one is a good public speaker or one's inborn skill is public speaking, that person's interest will also be in those professions or work that involves public speaking. Similarly, if one's passion is acting or performing stage shows, that person would naturally have acting as an inborn skill. He or she would do very well in professions that involve acting. Passion is always linked to inborn skill. If someone has passion for singing, that person's natural skill can be easily said to be singing and vice versa. Such is the connection between them. So finding our natural skills or passions is the first step toward finding purpose in life. This is because they are related and also our purpose rests on the foundation of these.

How Does One Find One's Interest or Passion?

Everyone has some interest or the other, generally outside his or her profession. This could be singing, acting, photography, music, fashion/interior design, painting, dancing, artwork, bird watching, or any number of other things. It is just that one has to analyze one's life to know what one's interests are, and God would have given the required skill to support that person's interests. This strong interest is also termed passion. Once the passion is known and if a career is made in the area of one's passion, then the work is no more mere work but rather a hobby that results in excellence. Self-introspection can reveal one's interest and a lot of other unknown facts about oneself, all of which are equally necessary to excel.

Determining Facts about Oneself through Self-Analysis:

From time immemorial philosophers across the globe have been advocating the need for self-awareness. There is a reason for this unanimity among them on the need for self-analysis. When practiced properly, self-analysis can help a person gain a lot of knowledge and find answers to questions such as:

- What are my likes and dislikes?
- What makes me happy or sad?
- How much food should I consume to stay healthy?
- What is my tolerance of liquor?
- How many hours of sleep do I need each day to remain healthy and invigorated?
- At what time of day does my performance peak?
- What are my interests in life?
- What am I passionate about?
- What comes spontaneously or effortlessly to me?
- What kind of music will elevate my mood?
- What do I really want to become in my life?
- What is the purpose of my life?
- What kind of exercising can make me feel fresh and healthy?
- How much do I need to exercise?
- What genre of movies do I like to watch?

And many more questions like these.

It is difficult to find answers to these questions, but it isn't impossible. All we have to do is start thinking about it when we are alone. Through repeated attempts to find the answers, we can get them. We do this analysis often to know about others but hardly make an attempt to know ourselves. Knowing ourselves will keep us within our limits and will keep us happy and healthy. It can also improve our relationships with others tremendously.

Self-introspection should therefore be our priority, as our success in life hinges on it.

Does the Purpose of Life Have Any Bearing on Health? If So, How?

Health is directly linked to happiness. People who have passion and love for what they are doing tend to be happy and healthy. On the contrary, when one is just doing his work for the sake of surviving in life, just to get paid so he can take care of his family, that person may experience stress, strain, disappointment, anxiety, etc., as they are all the result of having a negative outlook in life. Diseases such as diabetes, cardiac arrest, acidity, sleeplessness, blood pressure, and others are the byproducts of this negativity.

Are There Cases Where People with Purpose Made It Big in Life?

There are many success stories of ordinary people with extraordinary zeal to make it big in life. They all faced difficult situations, hurdles that anyone with weak determination would have given up and gone into hiding. If they succeeded at all, it was because of their burning desire coupled with strong purpose behind what they were doing and the passion for excelling in life.

Let us explore a few of them to know how they did it.

Rajiv Bajaj

Maker of Bajaj Pulsar,
the World's Most Profitable Bike

Prior to the 1991 economic reforms, scooters dominated Indian roads, and models from the Bajaj group (scooters such as Chetak and Super) ruled the roost. Customers used to order the scooters and wait for almost ten years to get them. People would do whatever was required to own their products. It was considered to be the middle-income group's aspirational vehicle. Those were the days when industries were under the government's control, and everything was centrally planned and executed by the government. For anything and everything, one had to procure licenses from the government. Hence, capacity constraint was quite common.

By the mid-1990s, the sales of scooters plunged as the consumers evolved and satellite TVs, Internet, etc., arrived on the scene. This changed people's aspirations and made them demand new-age products and services. This included cool-looking, trendy, and state-of-the art bikes, thus opening up a huge market for such products. Sensing an opportunity, international companies, such as Yamaha, Honda, and Suzuki, along with their Indian partners, launched fuel-efficient, 100cc bikes with super pickup. This pushed Bajaj, with its classic scooters as the main product, to the fourth position from number one. Sales tanked heavily, affecting profits. The company had a tie-up with Kawasaki, a Japanese conglomerate, to manufacture bikes. But somehow, there were lots of defects in the manufactured bikes, hence Bajaj – Kawasaki bikes could make no mark in the Indian bike market at all.

That was the time young Rajiv Bajaj with a postgraduate in manufacturing systems from Warwick University in the United Kingdom, decided to take the issue head-on and do something to change the shrinking market share of Bajaj products. He happens to be the son of Rahul Bajaj – Chief Executive Officer (CEO) of Bajaj Auto limited.

When he studied the problems, he found that the issue was with the attitude. With Bajaj being a scooter company, the founders never gave the required attention toward the manufacturing of the bikes, as bikes formed just 10 percent of the business in 1996. As a result, the bikes were not as fuel efficient as other Japanese models that were dominating the market.

There were also quality issues, as the manufacturing process for the bikes was outdated, and, simply put, the management at Bajaj was not mentally prepared for a change. They were doing it just for the sake of doing. It was a herculean task for Rajiv to convince the board of directors and even his father to give special attention to bikes, because the market for classic scooters was shrinking with the younger population preferring bikes to scooters. There was a push back from the board; its members' perceptions about Rajiv were that he was too young to understand market dynamics.

He proposed to break the collaboration tie-up with Kawasaki and build a bike from the ground up with young folks in mind. This too was rejected or opposed by the management, which was not mentally tuned in to the changed times and the market requirement of the Internet era. As the clamor for increasing attention toward bikes grew louder, Rajiv was finally given the task of developing a bike from scratch. Because he was facing issues related to perception from the founders from the beginning, he was under tremendous pressure to perform and build the right product the first time. No excuses whatsoever would be accepted if the product ever failed.

With his younger brother Sanjiv, who had an MBA from Harvard, Rajiv formed a crack team of young and motivated people to work on the bike project. To not be influenced by people who were working at their own slow pace at the existing factory, Rajiv proposed building a new factory in Chakan near Pune in the state of Maharashtra to design, develop, and manufacture the futuristic bikes.

Factory: In the new factory, Rajiv created teams of young engineers. Some were fresh from college and some had experience, but he made sure they were very young at heart and open to thinking and working differently. Most of them were bike enthusiasts, bike owners, or had a liking/passion for futuristic bikes.

They were taught to adapt modern Japanese processes for manufacturing, quality, and sourcing. The result was that Rajiv's factory started looking like an MNC factory that could produce world-class products.

Vendors: Before Rajiv took up this responsibility, he found that Bajaj had more than one thousand vendors, and only a few of them produced quality products. He pruned the number of vendors to two hundred and encouraged them to invest in the latest technologies. Suggestions were made to them by Rajiv to adapt modern manufacturing processes in order to achieve product quality consistently. With firm assurances from Rajiv that he would buy their products, the vendors made the required attempt to raise the product quality phenomenally high.

Dealers: The dealers who were selling Chetak scooters in India had been doing so for decades and were tuned to selling and servicing them. Most of the vendors eventually became arrogant, because Chetak models were selling like hotcakes. Customers were lining up to place orders to buy Chetak scooters on a daily basis; they had to wait five to ten years to lay their hands on their scooters. Such was the demand for them. Because of all this, the dealers showed the least interest in selling Bajaj bikes designed by Kawasaki, as the volume of the bikes was low. As a result, bike sales were languishing.

Rajiv noticed this and wanted to change that culture. He realized that for Bajaj to succeed in the new millennium, it had to be customer centric. The dealers' arrogance was not tolerated anymore. He pruned the dealer network and picked those who had the attitude and infrastructure to service all the products from the Bajaj group with care.

Research and Development: It was important to find someone to head Rajiv's newly set up R&D department. This person needed to be young and have faith in Indian talents. Rajiv zeroed in on Abraham Joseph, a mechanical engineer from the Regional Institute of Technology. Rajiv believed that R&D doesn't require old, experienced people with gray hair but people with a lot of passion and imagination. His belief was strengthened when he visited Kawasaki R&D in Japan, where he found that its R&D team was very young and enthusiastic. Its R&D could come out with impressive, sturdy, innovative, and futuristic products with their young employees. Rajiv realized that if young Japanese workers could create magic in their R&D, equally young and ambitious Indians could do the same in India. He decided to build a vibrant culture driven by research and innovation at his company in India, which was so far lacking. He created exactly what he believed in. His team was composed of young, passionate, and enthusiastic people experimenting in his R&D department. This attempt clicked in its endeavor, and Pulsar was born.

How Pulsar Was Conceived: The marketing people surveyed young, aspirational Indian youth along with executives who were aged between thirty and forty. The result of the survey was very astonishing. These men wanted bikes not necessarily to commute between office and home or elsewhere. Instead, all they wanted was a fun-to-ride and powerful bike to flaunt that had contemporary looks.

This was contrary to beliefs during those days—that Indians always wanted fuel-efficient bikes just to commute. Another belief was that they purchased bikes because they couldn't afford cars. This belief was busted during the survey that put out the fact that they were even ready to pay extra if the bike was rugged with stylish looks and could be used for fun. With this input, the design department came up with eight to ten conceptual designs, out of which Rajiv and his team narrowed it down to three. They took these three designs to the youngsters in the town and noted down what they expected from Bajaj's new bike. Now the R&D folks worked on three variations of engines, out of which Rajiv selected one. He personally supervised the nitty-gritty of the remaining works, from the styling and painting to the design of the console, from the right kind of road grip that was required for the bike to the kind of spark plug to be used. All of these activities took twenty-four to thirty months to complete.

Finally, the new Pulsar was launched with two variants in November 2001—one with 150cc engine and the other with 180cc. It became a rage among the youth, and the bike attained cult status immediately. It was a runaway success.

When the owners of other bikes were talking about fuel efficiency, the owners of Pulsar were already talking about performance—torque, pickup, power-to-weight ratios, and much more.

For them, Pulsar was not just a bike for transportation but a relationship between man and the machine.

Under the leadership of Rajiv, Bajaj Company has launched advanced versions of Pulsar once every two years since 2001. All of them had improvements over their predecessors and became hits with the customers. Each one of them bagged awards from auto rating agencies. In fact, Bajaj launched its latest, most sophisticated, state-of-the-art bike called Pulsar 220NS in 2012, and it has already set the market on fire. Customers are giving good feedback about the performance of the bike. That is a good sign.

Rajiv is known for his outrageously big dreams. He is now working on some futuristic products. For example, a 350cc technologically advanced bike, which he intends to launch in 2015, as it is still under a work-in-progress state in his R&D department. Another product that Rajiv is proud of is his 100cc bike with best-in-the-class features and the industry's most advanced fuel-efficient engine, which he plans to launch soon.

Recognition for Rajiv and his team's hard work came when their work was appreciated in other countries, and buyers placed huge orders. In the span of a decade, he turned his passionate baby, the Pulsar, into the world's highly profitable bike with more than 20 percent net profit on each bike sold. And his company Bajaj Automotive became the world's third-largest motorcycle maker and an Indian auto company that exports a third of its production. Now Bajaj Pulsar sells in more than thirty countries.

It is an amazing achievement from a boy whom everyone considered just a kid in the beginning.

How Was the Purpose Linked to the Making of Pulsar?

A young and restless Rajiv wanted to create something that would change the course of history. He was not happy with his father's age-old Chetak scooter and wanted something new from the Bajaj group that could change the identity of the brand itself. He knew that the people out there were young and would appreciate something that met their aspirations and would be in sync with the times. What better product than a futuristic-looking bike that was rugged, fun to ride, and cool to flaunt? That was how the seeds of Pulsar were sown.

The management of Bajaj, including Rajiv's father, was opposed to the idea. When Rajiv repeatedly appealed to them to give him a chance to prove his point about bikes, it was finally given but awarded as a pilot project. Because of this, Rajiv had only one chance, and he had to do it right—the first time itself. He did a lot of things from scratch, such as building competent teams, building the required factory space, and getting the equipment for building the bikes.

He had suggested to the management that he would want to break the technology tie-up with Kawasaki and instead design the bike indigenously. This required lots of guts, self-belief, and confidence to begin with. He could not have achieved this without a clear purpose behind what he was attempting, and the purpose showed him the clear way to achieve his goals. Another purpose could be to eventually make Bajaj one of the top two profit-making companies in India.

Rajiv demonstrated that one can achieve anything one wants, provided one has a sound purpose behind it, has a passion for doing it, and is ready to work hard. It was amply demonstrated in his life.

Awards and Recognitions

Rajiv's hard work and late nights bore fruit when he finally launched his dream baby, Pulsar, in 2001. Customers gave a thumbs-up, and reviews gave positive feedback about the bike. The bike became the fastest selling in that segment in 2001–2. All the later versions have bagged awards from plenty of auto rating agencies, and there was no dearth of appreciations from people from all walks of life. His success story has been discussed as a case study in many B-schools in India.

For details, see: http://www.bajajauto.com.

Mr. Rajiv Bajaj, managing director of Bajaj Auto

Bajaj Pulsar 220 NS

BHASKAR BHAT

The Man behind the Transformation of Titan from a Small Watch Outfit to the World's Fifth-Largest Watch Company

C irca 1985, the Indian economy was in the iron grip of the government, which controlled everything from what India wanted to produce to what Indians had to consume. The government even had a say over who would produce what and how much. Its assessment was never based on market realities but decided arbitrarily. This resulted in supply constraints for a few decades till 1991. That was when Manmohan Singh, the then finance minister under the Narasimha Rao government, unveiled big bang reforms to loosen the economy from the tight clutches of the government. These reforms not only gave corporations and individuals the freedom to decide what products they wanted to produce and sell but even the quantity to be produced. Till 1991, it was only the government-owned agencies like Hindustan Machine Tools (HMT) in Bangalore and Allwyn in Hyderabad that could manufacture and sell mechanical watches to more than one billion people – population of India.

For those government agencies it was a seller's market. Whatever was produced, there was a ready buyer. No marketing was needed for their products, and there wasn't much technological innovation; hence, there wasn't a big variety of watches to buy. Even the people's intention of buying watches was just to know and keep track of time and nothing beyond that. So, whatever variety of watches was available in the market was enough for the consumers. In 1985, the government, under the leadership of the late Rajiv Gandhi, the then prime minister of India, had given a small amount of leeway to corporations to enter into foreign collaboration to produce goods made in India.

In such circumstances, India's Tata group started a small start-up company to produce quartz watches, which were hitherto not made in India. It tied up with Tamil Nadu Industrial Corporation (TIDCO) to set up a factory in Hosur near Bangalore under license from Casio, Japan. Initially, under the stewardship of Xerxes Sapur Desai, the company grew from nothing to Rs. 798 crore (US$150 million) in 2002. Titan was mostly making digital watches for upwardly mobile youth and had a market share of 60 percent. It could achieve this through branding, innovative packaging, and reach. The pace of growth and the dynamism of the company got a leg up when Bhaskar took over the realm of Titan in 2002–3 from Xerxes Desai. It was a watershed moment and a turning point for the company, as it suddenly became the most happening place. Bhaskar brought in professionalism with the induction of young and enthusiastic professionals from top management schools and engineering colleges. He even recruited people with arts backgrounds to bring in creativity. This brought newer ways of thinking and enthusiasm to work on fresh ideas.

Titan, under the leadership of Bhaskar, grew from a company that was one of the many small companies within the Tata group to be the fifth-largest company in profits and size within the same group by 2012. This is Bhaskar for the world—soft-spoken, intelligent, visionary, an enterprising leader, and, above all, a good human being. Under his leadership, Titan saw meteoric rise in revenues from Rs. 798 crore (US$150 million) in 2002, to more than Rs. 9,000 crore (US$1.8 billion) in 2011–12. Its net profit rose from Rs. 6.51 crore (US$12 million) to more than Rs. 600 crore (US $120 million) in just 10 years and is aiming for Rs. 14,000 crore (US$2.8 billion) in revenue by 2014–15. The company has aspirations and faces lots of hurdles, but Bhaskar believes it is achievable. It had a cash reserve of more than Rs. 1,500 crore (US$300 million) in 2011–12. It is a cash-rich company, whichever way one looks at it.

In a recent interview to the press, Indian stock investor and multimillionaire Rakesh Jhunjhunwala said, "I wish I could find the next Titan, but I do not see any on the horizon at the moment." He himself is a strong believer in the company and has a small stake in it.

Bhaskar's Accomplishments

The extraordinary performance of the company and its achievements can be attributed to Bhaskar's strategic thinking, meticulous planning, and hard work. To explain in detail, Titan's money-spinning jewelry venture, Tanishq, had 5,700 designs by the end of 2002. But the venture's creative genius got a shot when Bhaskar took over the reins of Titan, and by the end of 2011, it had more than 14,500 designs to offer customers, making it the largest branded player in the jewelry market in India, selling more than Rs. 7,000 crore (US$1.4 billion) of gold.

He ventured into the youth accessories division in 2002 and also made a big splash there. His brand, Fastrack, has already clocked revenues of Rs. 650 crore (US$120 million) and is aiming to meet a revenue figure of Rs. 1,000 crore (US$200 million) in 2013. Later, in 2007, Bhaskar started a prescription eye care division, Titan Eye Care, and expanded it aggressively into the metro and minimetro cities. This division has reached revenue figures of Rs. 200 crore (US$40 million) in 2012. Titan got into the manufacturing of precision engineering products for aerospace, defense and high-tech industries in 2003, and its revenues reached Rs. 300 crore (US$60 million) in 2012.

Though Titan was started with the purpose to make and sell watches, its diversification into newer areas has given the great punch to its performance. No doubt, Titan is a darling of share investors. The man behind all these high-octane actions is Bhaskar, and the company's success reflects brilliantly on his capabilities and accomplishments. These divisions are doing exceedingly well, as the details given here will showcase.

Establishment of Tanishq Jewelry

Titan wanted to diversify into other segments, as watches alone wouldn't bring in much-needed revenues. Its natural diversification was into jewelry. This was because internationally, watches and jewelry are connected with gold-plated gift items. The company entered this segment in the mid-1990s with the purpose of making a difference in the market and creating a Pan-Indian identity. It wanted to achieve this by offering something unique to customers.

Traditionally, India is a gold-loving country, and Indians consume the world's second largest quantity of gold from the international market (more than one thousand tonnes annually). The Indian jewelry market has always been fragmented with lots of local jewelers dominating the scene. To get into the unorganized market, Tanishq had to distinguish itself from others. Its distinction was that it would not enter the already crowded wedding jewelry market but instead concentrate on other segments with its trendy, stylish, and international designs; even its showrooms' ambience would reflect its young-at-heart and trendy attitude. Its design team created more than 14,500 designs by the end of 2012. This was an attempt to impress customers with sheer variety, making Tanishq a giant-sized branded jeweler that offered the largest number of custom-built designs to customers. Even gold-plated watches were crafted for connoisseurs.

The advent of Tanishq into jewelry retailing brought some standards into the jewelry retailing industry in India, which was very rare in those days. One of the standards was that of setting up a karat meter in every retail store so customers could check the quality of their gold and diamonds before buying. The karat meter used X-rays to give an accurate reading of the constitution of gold in their ornaments within three minutes. The idea of karat meters did wonders to Tanishq's credibility. Customers were encouraged to buy only if they were satisfied with the purity of the gold and diamonds at the Tanishq store. This boosted customers' confidence in their gold, resulting in more people queuing up to them.

Another standard the company set was that the employees (store salesmen/women) were treated on par with the regular employees of the Tata group, giving them the same benefits. The practice earlier was to hire people on short-term contracts to deprive them of long-term benefits and save money. Because of this, talented people were not opting to work in the stores, and those who opted to work were there as a short gap arrangement. Tanishq's move was appreciated and attracted talented people in droves, especially the young folks. These youngsters joined Tanishq with the aim to make their careers there. This made a difference for Tanishq, as selling lifestyle products like jewelry requires special skills. These talented salespersons helped Tanishq achieve great strides in the Indian jewelry market.

When the price of gold was going up, it became unaffordable for most Indians. The female customers of such families felt they wanted to wear jewelry that was affordable, yet didn't look cheap.

This was an opportunity spotted by Bhaskar, and he launched gold-plated jewelry with innovative and fashionable designs for girls and ladies who are young at heart. These gold-plated ornaments looked posh and elegant and were well taken by the youngsters. His attempt was a hit with them. By the end of 2011, Tanishq became India's most sought after jewelry brand among the youth with its exquisite range of 24-, 23-, 22-, and 18-karat gold jewelry studded with diamonds and colored gemstones.

Bhaskar now started focusing on selling high-margin, expensive jewelry with the intention of boosting profits further. He introduced highly specialized, handcrafted jewelry, along with diamond-studded pieces to the customers. They commanded a premium at Tanishq stores. These jewelry ornaments fetched a return as high as 26 percent on every rupee invested, making it a juicy deal. Bhaskar is now focusing more on selling such designer jewelry and eventually pushing the margins to 40 percent. All the initiatives he undertook were with a clear purpose and objective in mind, which finally yielded much anticipated results. Tanishq's traditional and contemporary designs worked magic with the customers, achieving the highest brand recalls while bringing in revenues worth Rs. 7,000 crore (US$1.4 billion) in 2012.

Establishment of Fastrack Division

By 2002–3 India was witnessing high growth rate with its newfound confidence in the service sector (IT services), whose turnover by then had crossed over US$50 billion. With the average age of Indians being less than twenty-five years old, that age group formed the key consuming class for products and services in India. Their interest in style was different from that of their parents, and Bhaskar realized that his next phase of growth would come from catering to this segment. Thus, he began experimenting with sporty, yuppie, and trendy youth fashion accessories through a separate division called Fastrack. This category included cool-looking sunglasses, leather waist belts, wallets, bags, college accessories, jackets, stylish wristwatches, etc., for young male and female customers. His bet paid him handsomely, and it apparently became the company's blockbuster success, as it was for the first time that a well-known corporate had ventured into that segment. People lapped up these products as if there was no tomorrow. With the majority of the Indian population being less than twenty-five years old, there is still tremendous opportunity for Bhaskar to tap. It may not be a surprise if the Fastrack division becomes as big as Tanishq one day.

Rise of Stature of Titan Watches from Local Watch Assembler to an International Brand

By 2010, rich Indians got into the habit of buying luxury Swiss-made watches from overseas, and Bhaskar felt the necessity to be in that segment too. He sourced famous, internationally reputed watches like Hugo Boss, Tommy Hilfiger, FCUK, and others. He created a separate retail premium venture called Helios and started selling these watches at five-star hotels, malls, etc. This venture too brought success to Titan. Also, in 2011 Titan bought a three hundred-year-old Swiss heritage watch brand named Favre–Leuba and started selling in India as Titan's luxury collection. This made Titan cater to all the segments of society with more than 1,200 types of designs. Titan has one of the most talented and motivated design teams in India.

Titan used marketing muscle to aggressively expand its stores in India and overseas, pushing the sales higher. As a result, Titan is able to sell more than 14 million watches in 2012 through 1,500 outlets across the world. Bhaskar proudly says that every three seconds someone, somewhere in the world buys a Titan watch. In the world of selling lifestyle products, keeping the customers' excitement high with the launching of newer products is the key to success. In line with this belief, the company showcased to the world HTSE-based watches that have been developed in-house. The term HTSE means high-technology self-energized mechanism, which runs on light. These watches can be charged using light as low as 200 Lux (measuring units). That means they can be charged using even candlelight. They draw inspiration from some of the self-energizing equipment used by NASA and other space agencies in their satellites. This was a kind of rocket science technology used in India for the first time by any consumer-durable company.

The ingenuity of Titan came to the fore in 2002 when it designed Titan Edge, the world's thinnest wristwatch with a quartz movement measuring an incredible 1.15 millimeters in thickness. The thinnest movement in a casing of 3.6-millimeter thickness became the world's slimmest watch. This attempt made Titan beat its archrival, Swatch, a Swiss watchmaker and holder of the world record for making the world's thinnest watch at a 3.95-millimeter thickness. This showcased India's precision manufacturing prowess to the world and gained worldwide recognition for its innovative and state-of-the-art watches. Bhaskar's consistent effort and passion resulted in Titan becoming the world's fifth-largest watchmaker by the end of 2011, and this is his major accomplishment.

Establishment of Titan Eye Care

India's population is more than one billion, and if even a fraction of it needs good eye care products and services, it still is a big and lucrative opportunity. The Indian eye care business was fragmented with no Pan-Indian brand. Also, because of this, the quality of products and service depended on where the customer resided. Customers in metro cities had access to better products and services compared to those living in small cities. There was a clear and visible gap.

With its new eye care division, Titan wanted to bridge this gap by making quality eye care products accessible to customers across India. It started its prescription eye care division in 2007, and it already has more than 250 stores and is still growing. Its success in this segment is attributed to having stylish and contemporary designer frames available at very affordable prices. The youth in India have tremendous aspirations to look and feel good, which is making them own more than one pair of glasses to match the color of clothes they wear. In big cities, some own three or more pairs of glasses, and there is huge opportunity for good products.

Titan has a lead when compared to the competitors and is making a lot of noise in this segment. Bhaskar is now strategizing to make Titan Eye Care as successful as his watch and jewelry division in the coming years. It will not be difficult for him when one looks at the rising demand the burgeoning middle-income group has in India.

So, what's next? Maybe perfumes or spirits. The world over, almost all the reputed lifestyle product companies are into these categories too.

Establishment of the Precision Engineering Division

Bhaskar realized that by bringing success to Titan watches and Tanishq divisions, his team had learnt the art of making precision products. He wanted to exploit this and tap the existing opportunities through a separate division. As a result, Titan Precision Engineering was established in 2003, catering to demand from diverse sectors. In those days, very few government departments had the skill to make micro precision products. Titan was the only corporate house to possess it. The experts from this division designed and developed

TSRF silver Nano filter for Tata Swach (the world's cheapest water purifier). Titan received accolades for its work, and this opened up more opportunities for it. This division has brought in revenues of Rs. 300 crore (US$60 million) in 2012, supplying components to MNCs and Indian customers.

Is There a Clear Purpose behind His Phenomenal Achievements?

For Titan, from just a small start-up wristwatch assembling company in 1985 to becoming the world's fifth-largest watchmaker in a span of twenty-five years, the journey was not easy. In fact, Titan group has transformed into India's largest lifestyle company, giving healthy competition to international ones in India.

Every work, be it establishing and transforming Tanishq into the largest branded jewelry company, setting up of the eye care division, or creating the precision engineering division, had clear purpose behind it. Strong purpose showed Bhaskar the way toward his goals; he knew what he was doing and why he was doing it. A lot of sweat, hard work, pain, and sleepless nights have gone into the success of the company. This would not have been possible without a burning desire and passion in what he was doing. Bhaskar had all these in abundance; hence, he accomplished it finally.

For details on Titan watches, see: http://www.titanworld.com.

For details on Tanishq jewelry, see: http://www.tanishq.co.in.

For details on the Fastrack brand of youth accessories, see: http://fastrack.in.

For details on Titan Eye Care, see: http://www.titaneyeplus.com.

Bhaskar Bhat, managing director of Titan Industries in Bangalore

Tanishq—India's largest jewelry
brand

Titan Edge—the world's slimmest
watch

Anand Mahindra

The Man behind the Transformation of Mahindra & Mahindra, a Local Company, into a US$15 Billion Global Conglomerate

If there is a company that has made people sit up with admiration and take notice, it is Mahindra & Mahindra (M&M), for its resilience to come back with a bang. The story goes like this: Before the partial opening up of the Indian economy to foreign companies in the early 1990s, the government controlled anything and everything. The economy was closed with a lot of barriers for foreign companies to come and sell their wares in India. This gave Indian businesses a sense of security that they had no real threat from the competition, as getting licenses for making competitive products in India was very cumbersome and difficult. The government wouldn't allow that. Because of this, companies simply had to continue producing and didn't have to fear losing market share. The customers were there to lap up their products. There was absolutely no incentive for innovation, product upgrades, etc. Indian companies had a royal time then, and the heavenly feeling continued till the mid-1990s when the onslaught of products and services from foreign firms began.

The old products that Indian companies were so proud of earlier suddenly started looking very obsolete, creating some kind of inferiority complex in the makers. From nowhere, the Coca-Colas, Pepsis, and Pizza Huts of the world started dominating the market. This resulted in some Indian products being sold to foreign firms, while others just stopped producing.

Here is a small list of those yesteryear companies and their products:

- Thumbs Up and Limca brands were sold to Coke.
- Premier Padmini, makers of the 1964 version of the Fiat 1100 Delight, ceased production in 2000.
- Hindustan Motors, makers of Ambassador cars under license from Morris Oxford, has produced cars from 1954 till the present date. However, hardly any new cars are seen as of 2012, as it is unable to compete with new technologically advanced cars.
- M&M, makers of the famous Willy Jeeps since 1949 under license from Chrysler, had to stop manufacturing the Jeep by 2000 due to technical obsolescence and was unable to meet the Indian government's safety guidelines.

And the list goes on. There are many such companies who either went bust and disappeared or reappeared in different avatars. One such company was M&M. Its turnaround story can inspire many.

In 1991, Anand Mahindra was a thirty-six-year-old executive with lots of aspirations, confidence, guts, and a can-do attitude when he was appointed deputy managing director of M&M. He became the force that brought in the transformation to M&M. He was instrumental in diversifying M&M into real estate, industrial infrastructure, aerospace, IT, and defense. He expanded M&M's automobile offerings.

Anand received countless recognitions and awards for his achievements. The most recent was conferred by US India Business Council (USIBC), which gave both Anand and also Ford Motor's Allan Mulley global leadership awards for their contribution to furthering the American and Indian growth story. When India opened up its economy for foreign investments, a lot of overseas firms flooded the market with state-of-the-art products. There was a lot of anxiety and confusion among Indian corporations regarding whether to stay on with the business or sell it and do something else. In such a scenario, Anand, with lots of guts and fire in his belly, came forward to give M&M a clear direction and show it the way forward.

He performed SWOT analyses of M&M. SWOT indicates strengths, weaknesses, opportunities, and threats. The result of this analysis clarified M&M's strengths and weaknesses with the opportunities that existed in India. It was found that though M&M was not new to the automobile segment, it lacked modern and efficient manufacturing systems and technologies. Building the domain from scratch would have been time consuming and difficult; what was needed was to quickly bridge this gap by forging a collaboration with Ford Motors. At that time, in 1995, Ford was looking for a tie-up with an Indian company to produce cars. However, the partnership didn't endure for long, as the Ford Escort failed in the market. The relationship soured, and the companies separated.

But for Anand and his three hundred-member team who worked hard, it was a learning experience that turned out to be a treasure trove for them. If it were not for Anand's audacious decision to design, develop, and engineer a world-class car from scratch in India, the team would have dispersed and gone elsewhere. There was so much excitement in the team after Anand's decision, because whatever they were about to build had not been attempted in India previously. It was the same team that was finally responsible for designing, manufacturing, and delivering the completely Indian-made utility vehicle Scorpio in 2002.

Pawan Goenka, who came from General Motors (GM) in 1992 to M&M as the general manager for R&D, headed the team along with Allan Durant, who was then an executive director of M&M.

Much effort was put into selecting suppliers that were very forward thinking and aspirational like Anand. They were encouraged to design and develop their products on their own. When required, Mahindra encouraged them to have foreign collaborations to be on par with the technology needed.

Mahindra developed the diesel engine through its in-house team with help from AVL Designers in Austria. The petrol engine was sourced from Renault. For other things, Mahindra's design team handed over requirements in the form of specifications to the suppliers, and the suppliers had to do the rest. For instance, the suppliers were responsible for designing, developing (engineering), testing, and validating the parts they manufactured. Later, when the parts were done with testing and validation, they were brought to Mahindra's factory and assembled there. This was how, part by part, an entire vehicle was built—from concept to reality without much cost and fanfare but with 100 percent supplier involvement. The suppliers had as much riding on them as Mahindra did, so they were as serious and as keen as Mahindra to make the vehicle a grand success. In case the vehicle bombed in the market, apart from financial losses, it would have taken a heavy toll on confidence and self-esteem of all the people involved in the project. As a result, there was palpable anxiety and stress at Mahindra's head office and at the supplier's base at the time of the launch.

The newly launched vehicle turned out to be a super success; all the automobile magazines carried favorable reviews about the vehicle, whether it was ride quality, handling, or performance. Their judgment was that the vehicle was a good value for the money. Thus was born an original Indian vehicle called Scorpio. It had achieved many firsts in its attempt—it was developed at one-tenth the cost (Rs. 550 crore or US$110 million) that a large manufacturer would have incurred and negated the notion and belief that automobile R&D could happen only in advanced countries but not in India.

This attempt put the spotlight on locally available, reasonably priced, but world-class engineering and talented manpower. As a result, lots of foreign automobile and engineering companies established their own engineering design centers (EDCs) to help parent companies design better products at affordable prices.

The rest is history. Scorpio was named Car of the Year by *Business Standard Motoring* as well as Best SUV of the Year and Best Car of the Year by BBC's *World Wheels*. The vehicle was exported to fourteen countries by the end of 2007, and it boosted Mahindra's confidence. The making of the Scorpio utility vehicle has even become a case study at Harvard Business School in the United States.

The Making of Mahindra Xylo

Brimming with confidence and pride after making the internationally successful utility vehicle Scorpio, Anand and his team started to think about something bigger and grander. This time they wanted to make a vehicle that could compete with the best in the world, because it is always the best that can compete with the best. Anand's team now had to encompass the best talent in all categories of automobile engineering. There was, therefore, a manhunt across India to search for talented people. The best engineers, scientists, craftsmen, etc.—numbering 160—were handpicked for the job. Surveys were conducted by experts in various cities in India to know exactly what customers wanted in a new vehicle.

Experts also studied and captured the ways in which Indians interacted with their vehicles, whether they were driving across crowded Indian cities or on expressways. Driving habits were also studied, such as honking, frequent shifting of gears with frequent use of clutch; eating, smoking, drinking, and mobile phone habits inside the vehicle; and listening to music and frequent changing of radio channels. They even studied the kind of luggage people usually carried in India.

It was decided that the new vehicle should make people's lives much easier while traveling. For example, because the gear has to be frequently shifted while driving in crowded cities, the gearshift and clutch should be as smooth and as effortless as possible. Similarly, usage of mobile phones, air conditioners, cluster-mounted radios, and all other small things that mattered to the customers should be as efficient as possible.

Later, this survey was carried out in some of the world's major cities. The objective was to build a truly world-class automobile completely from the inside out. It is like putting a customer in the center and building a vehicle around him. To bring in the best driving experience, the world's finest components were sourced and used from across the globe either directly or through their partners in India. To remove human-created inaccuracies while assembling the vehicle, processes were automated using robots. The manufacturing processes were also tweaked in such a way that inefficiencies/ bottlenecks were reduced to the bare minimum. These operations made the life of employees easier so that the vehicles would be assembled without much physical strain.

Testing and Validation

Building a vehicle sturdy enough to easily handle any situation is a challenge. It is even more challenging to build the vehicle to withstand all the harshness of the external environment by itself without letting the passengers experience it. The vehicle was ruthlessly tested on the harshest conditions possible across the globe. It was tested by driving on some of India's pothole-ridden roads during monsoons and also driven in Rajasthan's desert during the summer when the temperature crosses 50 degrees Centigrade. It was also driven and tested on the frosted lakes of Manali during peak winter season and in Leh in the upper Himalayas where the oxygen content in the air is low. This was followed with driving at 160 kilometers per hour on the world's best freeways to study the drive handling and also testing in the coldest regions of Europe where temperature falls unimaginably low. All these exercises were to stretch and test every inch of steel and rubber beyond their limits so that passengers inside continued to experience comfort.

Also, it was tested for durability, reliability, noise-vibration-harshness levels, crash worthiness, aerodynamics, safety, drive quality, braking abilities, etc., using the world's most advanced computer-simulated environment software. These tests happened in the virtual world. The attempt to build a state-of-the-art, luxurious multi-utility vehicle (MUV) was no ordinary feat for Anand and his team, which resulted in an extraordinary vehicle called the Xylo. It was launched in January 2009 with six variants and is considered to be the best MUV within the Rs. 10 lakh (US$20,000) range in India.

The hard work had certainly paid off. As recognition, there were awards galore for Xylo for its brilliant performance and customer satisfaction. Some of the awards conferred by reputed organizations and rating agencies include ET ZIGWHEELS, Overdrive CNBC TV18, NDTV Car and Bike, BBC Top Gear Family Car of the Year award, and *Hindustan Times'* Top Customer Satisfaction award.

The Making of the XUV Mahindra 500 Sports Utility Vehicle

The world over, among utility vehicles, the sports utility vehicle (SUV) commands a premium. The automobile titans of the world—Toyota, Volkswagen, Ford, Honda, BMW and the like, dominate this segment. Customers swear by their SUVs when it comes to reliability, dependability, and sheer luxury. Now, it doesn't take much to think about how difficult it would be for a relatively new kid on the block from a developing country like India to muster the courage to enter into this big daddy's exclusive club. There is a very good chance of being trampled by them if there is any shortcoming in the products. For this reason, it is better for the kid to wait till he learns the art of making defect-free products and fully prepares himself before entering this restrictive, exclusive club.

That's what Anand did for his new SUV called XUV 500. He waited till he perfected making MUVs by successfully launching his previous two utility vehicles in India and abroad. This was to gain entry into the club with a product in mind, designed for global customers. Any issues with the product would create negative publicity and would dent Mahindra's carefully built up image. The team took much care to see that it didn't happen. To throw some light on how Mahindra's XUV 500 happened, let us go behind the scenes for the interesting story.

After the success of Mahindra's second product Xylo, Anand wanted to create a global vehicle designed and developed for global customers. He planned to use Mahindra's design engineers in India for a change. This was to test their design capabilities, and the product, if successfully done, would change the face of India forever as one of the key automobile design hubs of the world. Though the earlier products were designed in India, their styling was done abroad by foreign teams. For example, their first product, Bolero, was styled in Japan, Scorpio was styled in the United Kingdom, and Xylo was styled in Italy. However, for the XUV 500, the styling was done in India itself, making it India's local, 100 percent designed global vehicle or the "glocal" vehicle.

The desire to start working on an SUV began in 2006 as the earlier vehicle Scorpio was doing well in India, but it was used as a pickup vehicle abroad and not as an SUV. That was not the intent of Mahindra. It wanted to change the perception of the brand globally by developing an aspirational, youthful, and fun-to-drive kind of SUV for global customers, but it didn't know where to start.

However, during the Paris Auto Show in late 2006, the ball seemed to have started rolling. Some of Mahindra's experts, who were present at the show, went to the stage of other car makers, such as Toyota and Ford, with a questionnaire to collect information about what they would like to have in a new SUV and took note. They interviewed almost 1,500 people across cities in South Africa, Italy, Spain, Australia, and India and prepared the needs-versus-want list.

When the data was mined from the elaborate database captured during the survey, one thing that came to the forefront was that people loved to drive an SUV that had an animal instinct—very very aggressive looks, powerful, and sporty, yet safe and easy to handle. The data was passed on to the design team, and they took some time figuring out the kind of design that could satisfy the customers. Because the customers wanted aggressive power with style, it was decided to capture this in the cheetah's looks, indicating it was ready to pounce. It was also decided that the SUV should have a monocoque structure instead of mounting the body on the chassis. Monocoque represents integration of the two, the body and the chassis, for better handling, good road grip, power (approximately 140–150 bhp), and high fuel efficiency. A clay model of the SUV was done and shown to teenagers, fashion designers, and artists to gather their opinions and feedback, as they could easily visualize trends in futuristic cars. The team developed the SUV with the customers' wants and needs in mind. The new SUV also has a customer-centric design, which means it is built around the customer's needs like the Xylo. Here too all the components were sourced from the makers of world-class products to maintain quality. No compromise on quality was ever allowed.

More than 250 prototypes were built and driven around 2.35 million kilometers across the cities of New Zealand, Austria, Sweden, China, South Africa, the United States, and India. The vehicle was also validated in Mahindra Research Valley (MRV) for more than two years on all the aspects of engineering. The tests were done in some of the toughest and most ruthless test environments. All the issues found during the tests were removed, and systems were perfected. In the process of developing the SUV, Mahindras filed more than thirty patents. They decided to aggressively price it, at least 15 to 20 percent cheaper than available SUVs in the category to lure the customers. Also, to make the offer juicier, some of the best features that are found in premium SUVs that cost more than Rs. 20 lakh (US$40,000) were packed in the XUV, making it irresistible.

Finally, in September 2011, Mahindra XUV 500 was launched in India. It received an overwhelming response from customers and reviewers alike. XUV 500 bagged twenty-two awards within just eight months of its launch, making it the highest ever granted for any vehicle in India. A few of the awards include Car of the Year, SUV of the Year, Viewer's Choice Car of the Year, and Best Value for the Money.

The XUV 500 found so much unprecedented success that Mahindra was unable to cope with demand. Bookings were temporarily stopped to clear the backlogs. The company had not anticipated demand of such scale, and its production systems were not equipped to take on the rush. In 2012, during the cyclical recession, the demand for automobiles was very subdued, but not for the XUV 500, as has been reported by India's financial daily *The Economic Times*.

Mahindra's Ssang Yong Motors' Takeover Story

With a series of successes and a never-say-die attitude, Mahindra now wanted to position its brand as one of the top-notch SUV makers of the world, competing with the who's who of global giants. With this intention and purpose in mind, the company set its sights worldwide on any existing companies for takeover. This was the best way to add to the portfolio of their products.

South Korea's bankrupt Ssang Yong was looking for buyers in 2010; Mahindra did a quick due diligence and found that Ssang Yong met its requirements. Mahindra took over the Korean company in late 2011. Financial analysts and experts hailed this move, as Ssang Yong had a good product lineup but was cash-strapped, while Mahindra had surplus cash but not that good of a product portfolio. Both the companies had sky-high aspirations. The chemistry gelled well, and merging happened.

This clearly indicates Anand Mahindra's intention to turn Mahindra into a world-class automobile company specializing in SUVs. The purpose is clearly visible in all of the actions he has been doing of late.

Establishment of Mahindra Research Valley in Chennai

Any company that wants to establish itself as an automobile giant should have considerable expenses incurred on R&D. It should not only be researching the technologies present now but also the ones that would come maybe five to ten years down the line. This requires a lot of investment, focus, hard work, and infrastructure to accommodate people who have the caliber to visualize and bring futuristic technologies to life. An automobile has many areas where cutting-edge research is happening the world over, for example, on futuristic engines, drive platforms, ride quality, alternative fuel, electronics, infotainment, fuel cells, material science, and drive-by-wire technology.

If there is one place that could house all of these, it is Mahindra Research Valley (MRV) in Chennai, built at a cost of Rs. 600 crore (US$120 million). This project was conceived in 1993 when Anand Mahindra, then a young executive, visited Chrysler's R&D in the United States. He was really astonished to see the way the center was built and how cool it was that the scientists were playing with the technologies of the future. He got a firsthand experience of what it takes to make an automobile giant and decided to have one built in India, housing all technologists with world-class infrastructure, sourced across the globe with even the test tracks to test and validate the vehicles.

Worldwide, the auto companies flaunt this kind of infrastructure to instill confidence in the customers about their products and also to boost their image when they are competing against other giants with similar infrastructure. It also signifies that the company (Mahindra) is a long-term player and a serious contender for them. As the saying goes, "The proof of the pudding is in eating," and the proof of the MRV acting as a game changer for Mahindra is, the fact, that the most successful XUV 500 was designed, developed, and validated at the MRV in Chennai.

Was There a Clear Purpose behind Anand's Every Move?

Yes, of course. Without purpose and intent, Anand wouldn't have moved an inch in his endeavor to transform Mahindra & Mahindra to Mahindra Rise, representing a company with youthfulness and enthusiasm, and be able to connect with young and ambitious customers of the world. If the story is analyzed carefully, one thing that comes to the forefront is that Anand was not all that keen to get into the car segment that had a good market. On the contrary, he likes to have Mahindra branded as a top-class, internationally reputed SUV maker. India's spending on infrastructure seems to be in the trillions of dollars in the coming decades. This will lead to huge demand for technologically advanced commercial vehicles such as trucks, pickup vans, and busses. Therefore, Anand forged an alliance with American truck maker Navistar to get into a fast-growing, heavy and medium commercial vehicle (HCV and MCV) market giving headaches to established truck makers like Tatas and Ashok Leyland in India.

Another milestone was the purchasing of Kinetic Engineering, the makers of Kinetic scooters in India. This signals the arrival of Mahindra into two scooter and bike segments. Though there were initial product failures, it has learnt its lessons quickly and has come out with a scooter called Rodeo RZ, which received good reviews from reviewers in 2012.

Mahindra is planning to set up an MRV kind of research infrastructure in Pune City (in Maharashtra state in India) to exclusively cater to two-wheeler research and technology development. It wants to invest a mind-boggling Rs. 500 crore (US$100 million) on that. Mahindra's rise and expertise in frugal engineering has garnered much news coverage abroad. The most recent people to be impressed by it are Taiwan's SYM Automobile Company executives, especially with the performance of Rodeo RZ. They were keen to source the technology to manufacture and launch Rodeo RZ in Taiwan's market. This is contrary to the trend that Indian companies always seek technology from foreign firms.

Under the stewardship of Anand, Mahindra got into the information technology arena through collaboration with British Telecom (BT). It bought over Satyam Computer Services (SCS) at a throwaway price after its founder, Ramalinga Raju, revealed to the press in 2009 that public money had been swindled and diverted for his personal usage. The stock price of SCS tanked, and clients and employees exited en masse.

Anand took over the management of such a scandal-ridden company. He formed a crack team composed of talented people who had the experience and caliber to look into Satyam's accounts. The team worked day and night under the leadership of Anand and other eminent personalities. Approximately three hundred terabytes of data was scrutinized; thousands of employees of SCS, the accounting firm PricewaterhouseCoopers (PwC), and others who were involved were interrogated. Issues were finally resolved after two long years.

The shareholders' and clients' confidence in a revamped SCS was restored at last. The employee exodus, which had begun when SCS made headlines for the wrong reasons, stopped and actually reversed. Financial analysts, government agencies, and others appreciated it as a phenomenal achievement. This made headlines again for the right reasons. The buying of SCS gave Mahindra what is called strategic breadth and depth in the IT segment. This turning-around activity reveals skills that a business leader should have. First and foremost, it demonstrates purpose and strong desire, intent, leadership skills, guts, management skills, and problem-solving abilities. No wonder then that it has been a case study at many B-schools in India and abroad.

Mahindra diversified into real estate, infrastructure development, finance, holidays, and even into defense. In 1991, the group turnover was Rs. 1,520 crore (US$304 million), which had reached Rs. 53,627.3 crore (US$11.5 billion) by the end of 2011; net profits jumped to Rs. 3,079 crore (US$516 million), making it one of India's cash rich and admired companies. From the day Anand got to the helm of Mahindra & Mahindra till the end of 2011, the share price of the company appreciated by a whopping 995 percent. It is unbelievable but true.

What an achievement for a company that was at crossroads during the early 1990s, and what a transformation now.

For details on the Mahindra group, see: http://www.mahindra. com.

For details on Mahindra Scorpio, see: http://www. mahindrascorpio.com.

For details on Mahindra Xylo, see: http://www.mahindraxylo. co.in.

For details on Mahindra XUV 500, see: http://www. mahindraxuv500.com.

Anand Mahindra, chairman and managing director of Mahindra Group

Mahindra XUV 500

DR. DEVI SHETTY

Excellent Cardiac Surgeon and the Man behind the World's Cheapest Cardiac Surgery

Twenty-day-old Samuel from Africa had a hole in his tiny heart, and his parents were obviously very worried and grieved. Their joy of having a baby came to a creaking end when the local doctor broke the news about the hole. They did not know what to do, because Africa lacked a cardiac-care facility for infants and kids. An expert in this field asked the parents to rush to Bangalore in India and approach Dr. Devi Shetty regarding operating on the baby. They did just that, and the baby was operated on at a fraction of what it would have cost them in Europe or the United States. After the surgery, the joyous parents flew back with the baby, with lots of good memories to share with others.

Similarly Maadayya, a young boy from Chamarajanagar town in Karnataka state of India, some two hundred kilometers from Bangalore, had been living with a hole in his little heart for five years. His father was a poor farmer and could not afford treatment in private hospitals. He approached government hospitals and begged the doctors there to treat his son, but because of insufficient infrastructure and funds, they could not do anything. He was very depressed and prayed to the almighty with full faith and hope. It looked like his prayers were answered. By chance, he came to know about the telemedicine facility available in the nearest government hospital in his town. He spoke to Dr. Shetty and found that Dr Shetty's team at his iconic hospital, Narayana Hrudayalaya, could treat his son for free.

He rushed his son to the hospital in Bangalore. Dr. Shetty took a personal interest and saw to it that the hole in the boy's heart was closed and the operation was successful. The poor father with his little son left the hospital with a heart filled with blessings for the doctor and with uncontrollable joy. For him, Dr. Shetty is not a mere doctor but a savior—a god in human form.

The list of such stories with happy endings is countless. Welcome to the world of Narayana Hrudayalaya, the brainchild of Dr. Shetty, a fine human being, an excellent surgeon, a shrewd businessman, and a compassionate gentleman. He is the man behind the Narayana Hrudayalaya hospital in Bangalore. His hospital does the highest number of cardiac surgeries in the world, at an average of thirty-eight operations a day. The mortality rate of his heart surgeries is at an impressive 2 percent and is lower than most of the private hospitals in the United States. It costs just over a lakh rupees (US$2,000), which is a fraction of what it would cost for a similar surgery in other hospitals in India and elsewhere. Though his hospital is famous for cardiac surgery, it is also known for cardiology, neurosurgery, pediatric surgery, hematology, nephrology, and ophthalmology.

Narayana Hrudayalaya is working on the concept of five thousand-bedded, multispecialty, well-equipped hospitals on the outskirts of some of the major cities in India. Here, all sorts of health-related problems can be treated. To begin with, the first hospital was set up in Bangalore with five thousand beds.

Dr. Shetty is on a mission to make world-class health care affordable to the masses. He says that even one hundred years after the first heart surgery was carried out, it still is affordable by only 8 percent of the world's population. He is interested in making health care accessible to the rest of the population by using innovative ways of technology. Narayana Hrudayalaya is known for its state-of-the-art infrastructure to treat nearly all kinds of human ailments. It made international headlines and attracted the attention of policy makers and management gurus when they heard that Dr. Shetty was treating poor people with high-class treatment. What is interesting to know is not what he is doing but how he is doing it. The curiosity is understandable, as the world over affordable quality health care has remained just a promise on paper; no one has been able to make it a reality so far. It is not that they do not want to, but they do not know how. Naturally, there has been tremendous interest across the world, and a lot of his work has been taken up as case studies at various universities in India and abroad, including Harvard and Wharton.

How Did Dr. Shetty Reduce the Cost of Treatment So That the Poor Could Benefit?

To begin with, let us look at some statistics. An average cardiac bypass surgery costs approximately US$25,000 (Rs. 12.5 Lakhs) in the United States and US$15,000 (Rs. 7.5 Lakhs) in Canada. In India, it costs between US$5,500 (Rs. 2.75 Lakhs) and US$7,000 (Rs. 3.5 Lakhs), depending upon the complexity of the problem. But at Narayan Hrudayalaya, it would always cost less than US$3,000 (Rs. 1.5 Lakhs), irrespective of the complexity of the operation and length of stay. Around 40 percent of the hospital's patients pay less than US$3,000.

Nearly 30 percent of patients use the Narayana Hrudayalaya-promoted micro-insurance *Yashasvini*. For every operation performed through this insurance, Narayana Hrudayalaya gets about Rs. 60,000 (US$1,200) as reimbursement from that insurance plan. Dr. Shetty makes money from the post operation rooms. He has semiprivate and private rooms to offer to the patients and their relatives. It would cost an additional Rs. 150,000 (US$3,000) to Rs. 200,000 (US$4,000), depending on the kind of room used during the patient's stay in the hospital. For poor people who are not covered by insurance, he gives discounts, and sometimes he charges nothing from the poorest of the poor. Such discounts and freebies are funded by the hospital's charitable trusts, individual donors, or sometimes from the hospital's kitty itself. Dr. Shetty's instruction to the team is that no one who comes to Narayana Hrudayalaya should be denied treatment due to lack of funds.

Dr. Shetty took all the staff, including doctors, surgeons, and others, into confidence that they would get salaries at par with what other hospitals pay. However, they would need to do more, as Narayana Hrudayalaya's mission is to bring the cost down and serve all kinds of patients, including the poor and needy, and still be profitable. They were all doing exactly that with the pride of serving God through humanity, yet get paid handsomely for it. Narayana Hrudayalaya has been profitable from its first year of existence in 2001. Care was taken from day one that operations remain cash positive to serve the masses. The hospital follows a unique way of accounting on a daily basis to know if the day went cash positive or negative. At the end of the day, how much concession can be offered to needy patients is decided for the ones who have not enrolled into their Yashasvini insurance scheme.

Exploiting the Size

Dr. Shetty used the clout of his hospital's size to bring down the price in the way Walmart does. Walmart proved that with size, it could bring down the price. The price of vegetables depends on the bulk volume at which they are bought. The vegetables purchased from farmers are usually transported to the nearest distribution center, from where they are distributed to various marts and neighborhood stores. The less the logistics cost, the less the retail cost at the nearest retail place.

Dr. Shetty brought this concept to the hospital, as the pharmaceutical companies and medical equipment manufacturers form 40 percent of revenue outflows for any hospital. Now, it required a hard bargain with these makers to sell their wares at a discounted price or install the equipment free of cost and earn money by selling the consumables. The vendor could make money by offering the service for their unusually large number of patients at a cost. The back-of-the-envelope calculations showed the suppliers that they could make more money by following Dr. Shetty's suggestions than by the usual selling of the equipment at full price to him. That's how he clinched the deal, as most of the equipment in his hospitals is both owned and manned by their makers. These vendors get their revenues from offering services to an unusually large number of patients.

To understand a bit more, let us consider the example of catheters, which are mostly made by MNCs and sold to hospitals in India through resellers. Dr. Shetty bargained with the catheter makers, showing them the volumes needed to carry out an average of thirty cardiac surgeries a day and was able to purchase them at a highly discounted price. Big numbers always matter for discounts.

Similarly, the blood gas analysis test could cost up to Rs. 400 (US$8) in any Indian hospital, forming a bulk of the intensive care unit (ICU) expenses for the patients. With twenty to thirty such tests, the makers of such analyzers could hardly pass on any discount to the hospitals. But at Narayana Hrudayalaya, it is the sheer number that plays a hard game. With two thousand patients taking such tests on any given day, it costs around Rs. 10 (US$0.20) per test in Dr. Shetty's hospital. The equipment makers are more than happy to house them for free and offer services to such a huge number of patients at a cost. They still make more money than just plain vanilla sales of the equipment at full price. Apart from surgeries, Dr. Shetty's hospital treats 2,500 people in the outpatient department on a daily basis. The high volume has brought down the cost in many ways. Even at reduced cost, the hospital makes enough money.

Instead of buying surgical gloves from India, Narayana Hrudayalaya imports them in containers from Malaysia saving 40 percent on gloves alone. The hospital has moved to digital X-ray machines from conventional ones, saving on the recurring cost of film. Most hospitals use CT scanners, MRI machines, and other machines for only eight hours, but in Dr. Shetty's hospital, these are used for fourteen hours. As the volume increases, the cost per test comes down.

Also, Narayana Hrudayalaya has become a testing and proving ground for some new equipment. If this equipment can handle the high volume of patients, which this hospital offers without any hitch, then they can do much better at places where the volume is not even half of what this hospital handles.

How Does Narayana Hrudayalaya Ensure Such a High Success Rate?

Specialization is Dr. Shetty's mantra for ensuring quality work. Everyone specializes in his work, and the specialization happens through a series of trainings that each and every staff member has to undergo. Each surgeon specializes in one particular operation—for example, in cardiac surgery, valve replacement surgery, brain operations, or pediatric surgeries. The sheer volume of operations ensures the surgeon is world-class at his work. Similarly, this kind of exposure makes each and every person an expert at his work.

Telemedicine to Reach People in Distant Places

Dr. Shetty has collaborated with the Indian Space and Research Organization (ISRO) to provide quality health-care services to distantly remote, rural people of India through an innovative concept called telemedicine using Internet connectivity. The telemedicine network was initially established to mainly provide cardiac care, as the number people reporting cardiac problems was high. It was later extended to include other health problems. As a result, ECG reports, audio-video data, CT scans, or MRI scans are uploaded from the locally available terminals provided in the local government hospital or health centers by ISRO. The telemedicine centers use German-designed, portable ECG machines and similar equipment catering to all health issues to scan the patients and upload the result into the Internet with no hassles.

At Narayana Hrudayalaya, doctors on duty will get the report within minutes of its uploading. They then analyze the images and talk to the local doctors and patients to discuss what needs to be done with respect to treatment. They can advise the patients remotely from the Bangalore center. The hospital has also established five ICUs and twenty telemedicine centers providing consultation and support 24/7 to remote patients. More than fifty thousand patients have been treated in the span of ten years in this mode. The ISRO telemedicine network has now expanded to cover 332 hospitals—299 remote/ rural/district hospitals/health centers connected to thirty-three major hospitals across major cities in India. The network even works in remote parts of Malaysia, Mauritius, Pakistan, Bangladesh, and sub-Saharan Africa.

What Is the *Yashasvini* Insurance Scheme, and How Does It Work?

If Dr. Shetty has achieved his mission of giving quality health-care services to poor people at all, it is through the revolutionary micro-insurance plan called *Yashasvini,* which is considered the world's cheapest insurance plan exclusively catering to the poor. This plan has been conceptualized by Dr. Shetty, who gave life to it by roping in the Karnataka government, or KoG (Karnataka is an Indian state; Bangalore is its capital city) to reach out to various cooperative societies in the state. The KoG officially launched the landmark *Yashasvini* micro-insurance plan in 2003 with the objective of providing high-quality, low-cost health care to poor people by enrolling them into the scheme. Dr. Shetty and other philanthropists raised an initial corpus fund of Rs. 200 crore (US$40 million), and to that corpus, KoG added a significant amount to make the kitty bigger. Initially, it was started with the Karnataka Milk Federation cooperative society and later extended to other cooperatives, such as farmers' cooperative society, Grameen Bank, and handloom cooperative society.

An independent administrating body was established to administer the funds and invites bids from various hospitals to offer operation services at a rate set by the administrators. The other hospitals are showing interest in this scheme, because they are suffering from low occupancy rates, as their charges are high and only rich people can avail their facilities. These hospitals are ready to take up operations referred by the *Yashasvini* administrators, as not doing so puts them at a total loss. Spare capacity is best used by conducting at least some surgeries rather than letting facilities remain idle. These hospitals only perform operations and not any other testing or diagnostic work.

The *Yashasvini* insurance scheme covers free consultations and diagnostics at discounted rates, covering around 1,700 types of human ailments. The surgeries include the ones for the brain, stomach, gall bladder, spine, kidneys, and heart. The list of ailments is carefully prepared by studying the kind of health problems villagers generally suffer. The members can take benefits from more than one hundred fifty participating established hospitals, both government and privately owned.

The membership charges are as follows: for adults, Rs. 60 (US$1.20) per annum; for old people (50 years of age and above), US$ 2.4 (Rs. 120 per annum. The beneficiary does not have to pay anything if the cost of the operation is less than Rs. 100,000 (US$2,000) for a single surgery and below Rs. 200,000 (US$4,000) for multiple surgeries.

Extensive studies have revealed that only 0.08 percent of the population needs surgery in a year. So for every one million population, eight hundred people would require operations in a year. *Yashasvini* operates on understanding that out of one million members, only eight hundred need surgeries; the rest may need outpatient services, which are not expensive. The average cost of an operation is Rs. 10,000 (US$200), and the corpus required to cater to eight hundred operations is Rs. 8 million (US$160,000) annually. A premium of Rs. 120 (US$2.40) per annum per person and a membership in the millions will safely recover administrative costs, operations, and testing on the patients. It is essentially an insurance scheme wherein the premiums of healthy persons finance the sick.

Results of This Insurance Scheme

In the first stage, more than 1.6 million farmers had registered under the *Yashasvini* scheme by June 2003. In 2003, around 1,500 operations were performed. In the second phase, that is, by 2004, around 2.6 million farmers were enrolled under this scheme. Within the first two years, around 85,000 farmers availed medical treatment, and 25,000 farmers underwent various surgeries, which included heart, stomach, gall bladder, eye, and brain surgeries. Around 85,000 free outpatient consultations had been conducted by end of 2005, and around Rs. 200 crore (US$40 million) had been released to network hospitals for their operation and medication services. By the end of 2006, there were one hundred seventy-five network hospitals in Karnataka state alone, and negotiations were happening with neighboring states to introduce this insurance scheme. The phenomenal success of this scheme has become a case study of Ivy League B-schools, such as the Indian Institutes of Management (IIMs) in India and Stanford and Harvard in the United States.

Is There a Purpose behind Dr. Shetty's Frenetic Expansion of Hospitals and All His Work?

Dr. Shetty's only purpose in life is to make sure quality health care is made affordable to the masses, especially the poor, and yet stay profitable. Unless his hospital makes money, he cannot invest in good infrastructure and attract good doctors and surgeons. His hospital can attract patients only when the above conditions are met. Maintaining the balance among the three—that is, good doctors, world-class infrastructure, and low-cost health care—is really a challenge.

When he is using the volume of patients to bring down the treatment/operation cost, he has to make sure he attracts more patients. When patients are approaching, he has to remove bottlenecks arising out of shortage of space and beds in the existing hospitals. He has to either open new hospitals or enter into tie-ups with other hospitals in various cities to reach out to distant patients. It is required to make sure that the cost of health care remains low and affordable while Dr. Shetty's venture continues to be profitable. This calls for the brain of a genius and a body of steel to cope with such a challenge without getting stressed and exhausted.

In a television interview, Dr. Shetty had said that he is enthusiastic about working even harder as he is living his dream. He is never tired of thinking and talking about his passion. To expand his reach, he started building a low-cost, environmental friendly, one thousand-bedded hospital in Mysore (in Karnataka state), being built at a cost of Rs. 30 crore (US$6 million). Some of the best environmentally friendly concepts in building hospitals are being tried out in this hospital. If he is successful at building and affording a low-cost health-care institution there, he then wants to replicate this in all tier-two cities in the state and showcase it to other state governments to replicate his work. He is also establishing a two thousand-bedded hospital-cum-research center in the Cayman Island near Florida to attract patients from the United States, the Caribbean, and countries from surrounding regions. No wonder his hard work and passion has been recognized and rewarded—for all the contribution he is making to society. Some awards that have been conferred to him include the following:

- Padma Bhushan award for medicine by the Government of India
- 2011 Economist award for the best business process
- Honorary degree, University of Minnesota, United States
- Schwab Foundation award in 2005
- Padma Shri award for medicine in 2004
- Dr. B. C. Roy award in 2003
- Sir M. Visveswaraya memorial award in 2003
- Ernst & Young Entrepreneur of the Year award in 2003
- Karnataka Rajyostava award in 2002
- Karnataka Ratna award in 2001

A lot of people merely talk about doing something for society when they retire but never even attempt to begin such work. They give some lame excuses for their inaction. Here is a humble person with roots in the Kinnigoly village of the South Canara district in Karnataka state of India who walked the talk by making substantial contributions to society. Life, according to Dr. Shetty, ticks away with time; if it is not now, it can never be. No one has seen tomorrow, as death is completely uncertain. So he advises every individual to do something in his personal capacity for society before he dies.

It is better to live one passion-filled, purposeful life than a hundred lives without any. Life becomes even more worthy when that passion touches the lives of needy people by bringing them bountiful joy.

For details on Narayan Hrudayalaya hospital, see: http://www. narayanahospitals.com.

DR. DEVI SHETTY
Founder, Narayana Hrudalaya

KIRAN MAJUMDAR SHAW

The Lady behind the Making of Biocon Ltd., One of the Top Twenty Global Biotechnology Companies

I n the male-dominated world of business, it is difficult for women to make it big. It is even harder if the area of interest is something like biotechnology. The woman needs to have strong willpower (maybe more than a man) and consistently work hard to beat the clichés and achieve her goals. This was what happened to a young girl called Kiran Majumdar from Bangalore, a southern city in India, in the 1970s.

It was when India's economy was under the iron grip of the government, and society was inward looking and very conservative for a girl to even opt for studying the brew master course, let alone making a career in that field. One can imagine the kind of guts she must have had to try something that no other woman had tried and made it big in order to prove her critics wrong.

Kiran was born in Bangalore in 1953, did her schooling at Bishop Cottons School, and received her degree at Mount Carmel College. After completing her bachelor in zoology from Bangalore University, she took a brew master course from Ballart University in Melbourne, Australia, and qualified as a master brewer. She joined Carlton and United Breweries as a trainee brewer in 1974. She worked till 1978 and learnt the art of brewing from the master brewers themselves.

Kiran left for Biocon Biochemical in Ireland and worked as a trainee manager there. Men dominated in those days as brew masters in the breweries, and women were not encouraged to work in the field. This made Kiran think about going back to India to start her own venture with technical collaborations from Biocon Biochemicals of Ireland with a seed capital of Rs. 10,000 (US$200), mainly drawn from her own saved kitty.

Back in India, she had to face unsurmountable obstacles to do business, as business was meant to be a "male thing" in those preliberalization days. Banks wouldn't give loans, as nobody understood what she was doing and the word *biotechnology* was an alien thing in India. As a result, working capital was a real issue in her initial years. As per the norm, banks could lend only against collateral. The bank officials asked Kiran's father to stay as a guarantor and pledge his own house as collateral to lend her money, something with which she was not comfortable.

It was at a friend's wedding reception that Kiran met Canara Bank's then general manager Dinesh Nayak, and expressed her unhappiness about the norm. She argued that as per the bank's lending norms, the managing director should stand guarantee for the loan and not the managing director's father. Looking at the fire in her eyes and recognizing an intense desire to make it big in life, Nayak called her the next day and sanctioned a loan of Rs. 3 lakh (US$6,000), taking a personal risk. He was a very forward-thinking person compared to his peers at other banks. He was very appreciative of India getting into business in a new sector through a dynamic lady like Kiran. That was a turning point for her. She bought all the equipment and machinery from that money, and the real Biocon, the manufacturer of industrial enzymes, started off.

Next came the challenge of hiring people. No one was ready to work for a lady. Whoever came for the interview thought that she was a secretary, not the boss. This was because in those days only men could become bosses. Another problem in attracting talent was that she was operating from her father's car garage, from where people were uncomfortable to work. Kiran had installed the equipment in the garage office and hired some tractor mechanics to run them. Only those mechanics were willing to join her maiden venture.

Kiran borrowed approximately Rs. 14 lakh (US$28,000) from the Karnataka State Financial Corporation (KSFC, a finance company owned by the government of Karnataka) in 1979 and set up an R&D facility, along with a factory on the outskirts of Bangalore in Karnataka state of India.

Her venture, Biocon, started extracting an enzyme from papaya fruit and supplying to a company in the United States called Ocean Spray. Even today, forty years later, the company sources some of its enzymes from Biocon and talks highly about the products. Kiran proudly says, "It feels so good that we did all that, right in Bangalore, (India today – September 18 2011)."

In 1989 when she wanted to scale up a technology that she developed in-house, the KSFC was unwilling to lend Rs. 1 crore (US$200,000), as officials thought betting on the pilot project was too risky. They were only willing to lend Kiran the money if she licensed the technology from a reputed firm overseas. In 1989, Government of India mandated Technology Development and Information Company of India (TDICI) – a venture owned by Narayan Vaghul to fund new business ventures. TDICI had partnered with the Unit Trust of India (UTI) – a mutual trust company and ICICI bank to fund start-ups, and in fact, was looking for good business deals since then.

The company advertised in business dailies and based on that, Kiran took appointment and met Narayan. After she presented her business proposals, he was convinced that her venture deserves funding. He was enthusiastic about the potential of her pilot project and agreed to release a loan of US$ 200,000 (Rs. 1 Crore) with the condition that his company would acquire a stake in Biocon worth that amount and Kiran happily agreed to it. So, the deal happened in 1993.

In 1994 Unilever Biochemicals bought a stake in Biocon's parent company (Biocon Biochemicals, Ireland). It was an expression of confidence in the company and of the prospects its business would have in the future. The entire stake of TDICI was bought over paying Rs. 4 crore (US$800,000) within one year. Narayan's investment fetched multifold returns and he was very happy with it. With Unilever coming onboard in 1994 and with newer technologies, Biocon's business expanded very well.

Throughout the 1990s, Kiran perfected the enzyme process and was happy supplying to many companies abroad. At the end of the 1990s, the decision to change the course of her business from only enzymes to enzyme and biopharmaceuticals made her company's scale bigger in size. There was no looking back from then on. Her eureka moment, according to Kiran, came in 2004 when Biocon went public and listed in the Bombay Stock Exchange (BSE) subscribing thirty-three times. All her hard work and innumerable late nights finally bore fruit. She said, "It was an exhilarating moment for us", (CNBC – TV18 exclusive interview March 26, 2012). The joy was comparable to a mother seeing her baby grow up in front of her eyes and becoming successful in life with recognitions and adulation. A casual glance at the following numbers justifies her joy. Her company started with a mere Rs. 10,000 (US$200) in 1978. In April 2012, it recorded a turnover of Rs. 2,148 crore (US$430 million), a net profit of Rs. 338 crore (US$66 million), and a market capitalization of around a mind-boggling Rs. 5,900 crore (US$1.18 billion).

Every businessperson has his own traits that reflect the way in which he manages his business. Kiran's strong trait is at applying science with financial prudence to build Biocon's business model. Whether it is building the company's manufacturing assets, taking up research projects, or entering new markets, she does it only after an exhaustive study and takes it up only if it is financially viable. She realizes that when it comes to expanding to other countries or doing research in lucrative but high-risk areas, joining hands with others is always less risky. She could bring value to the project through the areas she was strong in and made the right moves in forging alliances with multinational companies. This shows her undying interest to remain profitable while strategizing her plans to expand into global markets. No decision would ever be taken carelessly if it affected the bottom line of the company.

She staunchly believes in the total revamping of the global health-care system so as to cater to the poorer sections of society. The current system cannot continue for long, as the system is skewed toward wealthy patients. There is nothing for the people at the bottom of the pyramid.

As an action of compassion, she has a stake in the micro-insurance initiated by Dr. Shetty of Narayana Hrudayalaya, which is cost effective and tailored for the poor.

She has also invested on research projects in her personal capacity to make cancer care affordable to the economically weaker sections of society. She proudly says that her company is developing a fusion protein that targets both the tumor and immune system simultaneously and kills cancer cells. The progress looks good on mice, and by the end of 2012, clinical trials have begun on humans and will take two to three years to know the results. If this research is successful, it will be a transformational breakthrough from "cancer care" to "cancer cure" and is expected to be much cheaper when compared to conventional methods of cancer care.

She also wants to strengthen Biocon's presence in treating diseases such as diabetes, cancer, and autoimmune diseases. The company is already doing well in the insulin segment with the diabetology division possessing a significant market share in India. Similarly, her company is striving to make a mark in other segments too, both in Indian and overseas markets. Biocon has a team of young and motivated research scientists in its R&D division. For a company that is research driven, these scientists are true assets. To monetize that division, Biocon has tied up with MNC pharma companies for joint research and is making good strides there.

Kiran has charted out a long-term vision for Biocon for it to be an Indian biopharmaceutical company with global aspirations and get into cutting-edge fields such as biotherapeutics to produce affordable drugs for the diseases. Her hard work to make Biocon as professional as any international biopharma company had borne fruit when Biocon was listed in the internationally reputed and elite *Science* magazine's top twenty biopharma employers in its 2012 survey. Her company was the only one selected from Asia. This points to where she intends to take her company in the coming years. At a time when most global pharma companies are eyeing record profits to keep shareholders and themselves happy, Biocon's emphasis on inclusive growth by producing affordable drugs for human ailments is appreciable. This shows her compassionate face.

Are All Her Efforts Purpose Driven?

The very purpose behind her hard work for taking Biocon where it is today reveals Kiran's strong urge for making Biocon a world-beater in biotechnology. Her phenomenal success and professionalism with which she operates causes many to sit up and take note. The fact that Biocon's board of directors and management team is full of professionals proves that the company is run professionally. It takes a lot of effort and imagination for the founders to decide how to run their company.

An organization can only attract and retain world-class talent when it provides them a professional working environment. Building such an organization is not child's play, and it requires burning desire, passion, consistent efforts, and imagination. In fact, Kiran has all that and much more. The very fact that she postponed her marriage and settled down in life during the late 1970s reveals her sacrifice. Kiran did what a sacrificing mother would do to her newborn with her newly founded company, Biocon, in 1978. When most girls her age were getting married one after another, Kiran was busy working hard to make her company grow bigger and stronger. It would have been impossible if her father hadn't supported her and shared her dreams. She married John Shaw when she was forty-four years of age.

In a free-wheeling chat with a TV reporter, she declared that Biocon wouldn't have existed had she got a job as a brew master in the late 1970s. Maybe she was ordained to start Biocon and give employment to many people.

Awards

Her hard work and sacrifice have been appreciated and rewarded profusely by society and the government. Here are some of the awards she bagged till 2012:

- Featured in Asia's 50 Power Businesswomen list (2012)

- Featured in *Financial Times* Top 50 Women in Business list (2011)
- Featured in *Forbes* list of 100 Most Powerful Business Women (2010)
- Featured in *Time* magazine's list of 100 Most Influential People in the World (2010)
- Nikkei Asia prize for regional growth (2009)
- Express Pharmaceutical Leadership award (2009) for dynamic entrepreneur
- Honorary degree of Doctor of Science from Herriot-Watt University, Edinburgh, and the University of Glasgow in 2008
- Honored with the Veuve Clicquot Initiative for Economic Development for Asia award (2007)
- Padma Bhushan award from India's president (2005)
- *Economic Times* Business Woman of the Year (2004)
- Ernst & Young's Entrepreneur of the Year award for Life Sciences and Healthcare (2002)
- Karnataka Rajyostava award

For details, see: http://www.biocon.com.

Mrs. Kiran Majumdar Shaw,
founder of Biocon Limited, Bangalore

HEMA RAVICHANDAR

An Architect of Modern Human Resource (HR) Policies of India

I f India's service industry has transformed from a kindergarten stage in the early 1990s to a force to reckon with by 2012, it is because of effective human resource (HR) policies.

What Do HR Policies Have to Do with India's Successful Service Industry?

Everything. Wrong or sloppy HR policy demotivates employees by bringing their productivity down, along with the company's profits. Keeping manpower leaner, meaner, and motivated is the responsibility of the HR department. The HR department achieves this through its policy, called HR policy, and is required to make the company churn out profits year after year. Also, the companies may implode and perish due to strikes resulting from a lack of trust between employees and management if policies are weak.

The recent (July 2012) killing of the HR manager of the Maruti car plant in Manesar in Haryana state in India, and subsequent damage to the plant by disgruntled employees, tells why the HR department should never be taken for granted by any company. The above event puts the spotlight on having strong employee and management relationships driven by trust.

Companies are realizing of late that there is much to gain by making their employees stakeholders in what they are doing rather than just treating them as workers who are paid to do a job. The right HR policy can make it happen and create an environment that motivates the employees to work hard and bring out the best in them. It can also build the sense of belonging in employees, which is very important for a company's success. This belonging creates harmony and happiness in the employees and the management.

Industrial relations, an offshoot of HR, has gained traction and has become one of the most sought after specialization subjects in HR management at leading master of business administration (MBA) schools in India.

The description given here sheds some light on how the HR department evolved from a nonglamorous one, with people sitting at a corner of the office doing low-profile, back-end work for the department at the center of the office doing crucial work for the company.

The HR manager calls the shots nowadays along with the chief executive officer (CEO) and others in framing all the company's policies. Suddenly, HR work has gained prominence.

Also, the story below narrates how HR policies have evolved from manufacturing-centric to services.

The Indian economy was mainly agrarian till the mid-1980s, as manufacturing was small and was not adding much to the gross domestic product. From the mid-1980s onward, manufacturing started looking up with the arrival of Maruti cars under license from Suzuki and bikes such as Honda, Yamaha, and TVS. Suddenly, manufacturing became the center of attraction for the young people to begin their careers.

In the manufacturing industry, workers use machines to turn raw materials into finished goods. Because of this, there was not that much scope for an individual's performance. Everything was happening either in an automated or semiautomated environment. Very little knowledge-based manufacturing was happening in India at that time.

The existing HR policies were more or less sufficient to cater to the workforce. However, when the service industry took off in the early 1990s with the arrival of IT companies, the environment changed altogether. The existing HR policy was not sufficient to handle employees doing new kinds of work. They were completely out of sync with the reality. The service industry was composed of IT, business process operations (BPOs), outsourced R&D, outsourced publishing, call centers, legal process operations (LPOs), and much more.

There were no policies to handle the following:

- incentivizing the hard work done by a highly educated workforce (men and women) working from morning till late in the night
- perks and salaries for people who travel overseas on short—or long-term contract basis on assignments
- the process of rewarding the hard workers/achievers and punishing the underachievers
- stock options for employees
- patent creation and rewarding the patent creators
- protecting women employees from sexual abuse
- women workers who have gone on maternity leave
- transportation and other perks, such as food allowance for employees staying until late in the night
- interbranch transfers on short—or long-term
- housing, personal car, and other allowances and much more that suit various types of industries that render services to overseas and Indian clients

A new set of HR policies needed to be written from scratch to capture the new kind of requirements these service-oriented companies demanded. It is still a work in progress, as the requirements are continuously changing to meet newer challenges.

A question may pop up in one's mind as to why these service folks are pampered so much. The answer is that for the new age industries, employees' intellect or knowledge becomes the raw material, unlike manufacturing. This intellect or knowledge is what goes into the making of products or rendering service to the clients. The better the intellect, the better the output. For this reason, organizations look for knowledge-based workers with above average intellect to run the show. There is intense competition to attract such people, and organizations go overboard to shower them with perks, as their profitability is dependent on the performance of such employees.

The intent of every organization, be it manufacturing or services, is to create a stimulating working environment that builds a bond among the employees and between employees and management. The intent is also to create an environment that motivates the employees to thrive.

It has been a serious challenge for the HR department to create a policy that enables it.

The organizations that do this successfully get into the prestigious list of Top 10 Great Places to Work. This list is prepared every year by a world-renowned ranking organization called the Great Places to Work Institute, which ranks organizations based on policies that enable relationships at the workplace.

An enduring relationship is established through

- trusting the people they work for;
- having pride in what they do; and
- enjoying the company of the people they work with.

It is not without reason that there is a mad scramble among HR managers to have their companies featured in the above list. Also, it pays to be in the list. First, being in the top ten gives companies the required visibility to attract talented manpower, as everyone wants to work for world-class companies. Second, there is a correlation between employee productivity and a company's profitability. However, productivity is directly linked to employee harmony, motivation, etc. So, to get to the list, the company should provide an environment that enables relationships, trust, etc., which, in turn, motivates the employees.

What Was Hema Ravichandar's Contribution?

Hema Ravichandar, an IIM Ahmedabad alumnus, was working at the Mico Bosch facility when she happened to meet Mr. Narayana Murthy of Infosys in 1992. She joined him at Infosys after hearing of his aspirations and the fire he had to make Infosys one of the best-governed companies in India. Infosys was just a 250-employee company with a turnover of Rs. 5 crore (US$1 million) when she joined as HR manager in 1992. By the time she left Infosys in 2005, it had an employee strength of more than forty thousand and a turnover nearing US$1 billion. Being the HR head, she framed new HR rules catering to the requirements of Infosys and introduced new benchmarks for HR practices.

In 2004–5, Infosys received a mind-boggling 14 lakh or 1.4 million applications for twenty thousand open positions. Hema set up a crack team of recruiters to process such a high volume of applications and fish out the best candidates for interviews. Tracking the progress of and offering appointment letters to selected employees was no joke. All this had to happen very efficiently with the least burnout. Her recruitment process is still alive and kicking even in 2012, though it underwent a few superficial changes catering to new demands.

Hema not only streamlined recruitment processes but also created new benchmarks for learning and development (L&D)—a simple and efficient process to make every employee enhance his knowledge through learning. She also standardized the compensation policy, taking into account the employee's experience and the area in which he possesses knowledge. If the person's knowledge was in a niche area coupled with good working experience, he would command a premium. Her compensation policy included work experience, along with deep knowledge in the subject to be eligible for salary at a premium. She standardized the salaries for various technologies, taking work experience into account. This made salary negotiation simple, as the interviewer had the data on hand during discussion to fix the salary. Later this policy became an industry norm, as more and more IT companies adopted it.

Hema devised a policy that creates good relationships between employees and the management by opening all the channels of communications. Another major contribution from Hema was to devise a policy to motivate employees. Studies have revealed that in any organization, institution, or government department, 80 percent of people contribute to only 20 percent of the output, and 20 percent of the people contribute to a whopping 80 percent of the output. The 80:20 rule is applicable to all companies. The challenge is now to identify those 20 percent that are the hardworking people and reward them handsomely. If the company is small, with less than one hundred employees, it is easy to find out. In a large company like Infosys, with more than forty thousand employees in 2004, it was a difficult task to identify and reward workers based on their performance. Nonrecognition of their hard work *or* equal treatment of unequals might demotivate employees. It was not an easy task to attempt. A lot of thinking, background studies, and pilot projects have gone into the making of this policy. Hema's policy had addressed the issue in an efficient way, though it is still a work in progress, as the situation is changing dynamically.

Multinational companies, such as IBM, Intel, and Texas Instruments, have provided employee share options (ESOP) for their employees as an incentive for working in their companies for some years. This is one of the ways to make employees stakeholders in what they are doing. This is a double-edged sword; it both incentivizes employees' hard work and makes the company reap the fruits of hard work through increased profits.

Hema implemented the ESOP concepts at Infosys in 2000. It was such an instant hit that it made waves in the Indian corporate circle and made huge media headlines too, as Infosys was the first company to do so in India. Later, other companies too followed suit. She introduced many more such policies that had become industry standards by 2012. A lot of companies have taken her policy concepts and improvised upon them as suits their requirements. She did future proofing of her policies so that they no longer depend on the individuals. These policies work irrespective of who is at the helm.

What Could Be the Purpose behind Hema's Hard Work?

The purpose could be to create an organization-wide HR policy that could motivate employees to do their best in creating and sharing the wealth among themselves, the management, and the shareholders. The policy was driven by good relationships through trust and honesty.

Under Hema's leadership, Infosys won several Best Employer of the Year awards in India and was featured in top one hundred rankings worldwide. Her work received wide coverage in HR forums and journals, resulting in accolades from the experts.

Hema is now an independent HR consultant for several Indian and multinational companies and sits on the board of several companies. She was formerly the chairperson for the conference board, the US HR council of India. She was a member of the national advisory council of the National HRD network of India and is a regular speaker at national and international conferences on HR. She gives guest lectures in leading B-schools in India.

Her achievements and accomplishments are really breathtaking and inspiring. She couldn't have had her path to the goals easily visible to her without knowing her goals first. Hema had to battle through the clichés, her opponents, doomsayers, and others to make her way toward the goals. It was not an easy task for her. For those who underestimated the power of women, she proved to them that she was a formidable force to reckon with and was equal or more capable than her critics. She achieved all this while being a wife to her husband, mother to her two kids, and daughter-in-law to her in-laws. This proves her excellent multitasking abilities.

She couldn't have begun her work like many other achievers without first knowing the purpose behind her work. After all her hard work and accomplishments, she certainly may be experiencing inner joy. This is because both are connected.

Awards and Milestones

- HR Professional of the Year award (2005)
- Outstanding HR Professional of the Year award, National HRD Network (2004)
- Lister, 25 Most Powerful Women in India, *Business Today* (2004)
- Lister, Successful Women Professionals of the Y, *Dataquest* (2004, 2005)
- Lister, 25 Hottest Young Executives of the Year, *Business Today* (2002)
- Led Infosys HR in India and in the United States:
    - *Business Today*, Hewitt's Best Employer of the Year—ranked #1 in 2001 and 2002;
    - *Dataquest*, Best Employer (2001, 2002), top five (2003, 2004)
    - *Business Today*, Mercer Best Companies to Work, ranked second (2004)
    - *Computer World's* Top 100 Companies to Work For (2003, 2004)
    - ASTD's Excellence in Practice Citation for Training Interventions
    - Optimas Award for Training Innovation for Progeon

For details, see: http://www.hrtrust.in.

Mrs. Hema Ravichandar, founder of HR Trust

T. V. MOHANDAS PAI

A Multifaceted Personality:
The Man behind the Rise of Infosys from
an Ordinary Company to One of the Most
Respected Organizations in the World

When we study the success story of Infosys closely, we see that there were a few key people who transformed Infosys from an ordinary company into one of the most respectable global conglomerates. The attainment of Infosys's iconic status has a lot to do with the following factors, among others:

- efficient corporate governance
- the way employees are treated and inspired at work
- the seriousness with which leaders are groomed
- the way it brands itself among the investor community
- the way it discloses all its financial transactions
- transparency in accounting
- the way it manages the challenges that arise out of cyclic boom and bust in the world economy
- the way it handles clients
- its values and the extent to which it sticks to them

Why Is It Important for Companies to Have Strong Focus on the Points Listed Above?

Companies are operating in a very competitive world, and the market is crowded and cluttered. In such a situation, there needs to be some distinction that separates the men from the boys. Those companies that focus strongly on the points listed above become elevated to a new league where there is a smaller crowd and where they can attract the attention and respect of the clients easily. Companies have to work on these points not just to make themselves special but for their very survival in the long run.

To explain: Good corporate governance is very important for any company. Those with good governance will have good processes, laws, customs, and policies that affect many stakeholders (such as employees, management, vendors, shareholders, bankers, the board of directors, and clients). It is an absolute necessity to have policies that motivate employees and build a sense of belonging in them. Similarly, it is important to manage and strengthen the bonding with other stakeholders through trust and honesty.

Once good governance is established, the company gets into a strong position from where conquering newer territories to generate revenues will be easy. Also, it can effectively address the challenges introduced by the competitors.

Companies the world over are aware of the advantages of good governance and do a lot of hard work to achieve it. Yet they struggle to achieve not even half of what Infosys has achieved. This is mainly because, from the beginning, the founders wanted Infosys to adhere to the values and virtues that they had in mind at the time they started the company.

Instead of just looking for profits at any cost, they accepted the profits only if it came to them through fair means. This kind of mentality in the founders is very rare. Though founders of other companies also wished to make their companies as respectable as Infosys, their efforts maybe did not reflect their wish. Those who put in a lot of effort may have retracted when the going got tough and profits were seen hitting the bottom.

Infosys founders were in a separate league altogether, because their die-hard faith and commitment to achieving their objectives in an environment that was fair, honest, and sincere toward clients, employees, vendors, shareholders, and society was highly commendable.

They did just that even in difficult times and won the hearts of many. Their investors, shareholders, and employees became both admirers of Infosys and its brand ambassadors.

As the saying goes, "like attracts like." Young Infosys founders attracted stalwarts like Hema in 1992 and T. V. Mohandas Pai in 1994 into the management team of Infosys. Hema became the HR manager, Mohandas became the chief financial officer (CFO), and Phaneesh Murthy became director of global sales. These are the ordinary people with extraordinary dreams and fire to make it big in life.

What Was Mohandas's Contribution to Infosys?

Mohandas, being a CFO, helped Infosys transform into one of the world's most respected and widely known software services companies. He formulated and implemented the country's first publicly articulated financial policy for the company. He played a key role in branding Infosys among the investor community and made the financial disclosures as open and transparent as possible. Infosys' annual reports under his supervision bagged awards consistently from the Institute of Chartered Accountants and from the South Asian Federation of Chartered Accountants.

Mohandas led the team that worked on the listing of Infosys shares on NASDAQ in the United States in 1999. Infosys was India's first company to list on NASDAQ, signaling the arrival of Indian companies on the world stage. Also under his supervision, Infosys completed the sponsored secondary offerings of American Depository Shares (ADS) in the United States on behalf of shareholders in 2003, 2005, and 2006.

Mohandas had even donned the role of HR director and was instrumental in conceptualizing and bringing out the world's largest corporate learning center in Mysore on a three hundred-acre plot, where more than ten thousand professionals are being trained annually as of 2012. Also, he is the brainchild behind Infosys leadership institute (ILI). ILI is touted as being on par with ones at GE, which has its corporate leadership institute in Ossining, New York.

Management gurus talk extensively of having second—and third-line leaders to work along with the main leaders; when required, second-line leaders can take over the overall management of the organization. The leadership transfer should happen without any glitch, and this calls for ongoing identification of employees who exhibit leadership qualities and then grooming them extensively to take up the role in the future. Infosys had that kind of foresight and, under the leadership of Mohandas, started the process of identifying future leaders. These future leaders were taken to a sprawling campus in Mysore to be groomed extensively for six months or so.

This way, Mohandas wore many hats in Infosys and was responsible for raising the stature of Infosys to an international level.

Did Mohandas' Hard Work Have Some Purpose?

Behind Mohandas's hard work there was a purpose to accomplish what the Founders had in their minds about Infosys. Under his supervision, Infosys achieved many firsts and made major headlines in the media. Infosys bagged many awards during his tenure, which lasted till 2011. Infosys was a publicly listed company in India. Its shares were listed in the National Stock Exchange (NSE) way back in 1993.

As soon as he became the CFO, Mohandas strived toward making Infosys different from other companies. As a step in that direction, he first brought financial discipline by making all the accounting transparent and slowly brought disclosure level to international standards. This was highly appreciated by the investing community, and the move brought respect for the company. With a portfolio of good clients, a dedicated team to execute projects profitably, and the company in the hands of trusted and honest management, Infosys became the darling of investors and the talk of the town.

This achievement did not quench the thirst for success. The founders this time set their sights overseas. They wanted to repeat their Indian achievements overseas too. For this to happen, they had to first increase the visibility of the company among the investor community there and subsequent listing on American Stock Exchange.

Infosys has been a publicly listed company since 1993 in India, and its annual revenues and profit reporting was as per Indian standards. For the investors in India, this kind of reporting is fairly sufficient. But to take Infosys to American bourses, it fell short of standards. The American companies, or those overseas companies that want to list on American bourses, have to make their accounting and reporting standards adhere to GAAP (generally accepted accounting principles). This was a herculean task for Mohandas and his team. They had to account for every penny coming in and going out—once in Indian standards for Indian investors and again in GAAP for overseas investors. To do this day in and day out is not easy for a company as big as Infosys, which has more than 150,000 employees, millions of shareholders around the world, and more than US$7 billion in revenues in 2012. The company's reputation would have taken a serious hit if it botched up with accounting and could even end up facing litigation for false reporting, which, in turn, may result in fall from grace.

Unless there is a dedicated team and a process to handle this kind of work, the entire effort is bound to fail. These processes should be tamperproof and should detect and report any process violations at the beginning itself. And above all, it should not be too cumbersome and tiring for people who work on it. Designing such financial processes is a rocket science, and only the best could do that. Mohandas is known for his childlike enthusiasm, prudence, and his foresight. Though consultants were involved in helping Mohandas and his team implement the GAAP at Infosys, it was under his supervision that the work was executed without any glitch. Later, with the help of experts, he got the processes designed, which could churn out the best, year-on-year.

In 1998 preparations for listing on NASDAQ was frantically on. There was not much time for people in Mohandas' team to learn leisurely and execute the work at their pace. The management wanted to list the Infosys stocks on NASDAQ before the end of 1999, come what may, as it would announce the arrival of India and Indians on the world stage in the new millennium. There was no looking back for the team; it was a do-or-die situation with lots of anxiety. The pressure was building up day-by-day, and the team worked 24x7 in shifts to meet the targets. Though war like emergency situation existed in the office, care was taken not to disturb the day-to-day operations, and it was business-as-usual for client servicing teams. However for people working on project to list Infosys shares on NASDAQ, it was not business-as-usual. There were no vacations or similar distractions for them till the goal was achieved. Everyone was busy contributing to the project with laser like focus. Mohandas led his team from front and made sure Infosys's shares finally listed on NASDAQ in 1999 as planned—the first Indian company to ever do it.

There was jubilation for Infosys for achieving this feat. Congratulatory messages were showered on the management from even the Indian prime minister and his bureaucrats. The successful listing on the NASDAQ got such wide publicity overseas for all its good work and high standards that CNBC had an hour-long program showcasing Infosys and its accomplishments and even interviewed the management. The market capitalization for its shares on NASDAQ reached a sky-high value of US$22 billion in 2006. Thus, the mission was accomplished.

Another achievement of Mohandas in 2000 was teaming up with Hema for the successful implementation of ESOP for the employees at Infosys. This involved hard work and a bit of a risk too, as the implementation should not take a bottom-line hit and also not affect investor sentiments negatively, thus bringing down the share price. Infosys was also the first company in India to reward its employees with shares. This was another feather in Mohandas's cap, as his achievement attracted accolades from all over the country.

Awards and Accomplishments

Mohandas's leadership qualities, his foresight, and his hard work were honored profusely.

- CFO of the Year by IMA (2001)
- Best CFO in India, *Finance Asia* (2002)
- Best CFO in India in the best-managed company poll conducted by *Asia Money* (2004)
- He is also working in the Khelkar committee constituted by India's Ministry of Finance to reform direct taxes.
- He has been actively working with regulators to improve the business ecosystem. For example,
  o he is a member of the nonresident taxation committee and is in the high-powered committee on e-commerce taxation constituted by the ministry of finance;
  o he is a member of the Securities and Exchange Board of India (SEBI);
  o he was a member of the empowered committee for setting up taxation information network (TIN) in India;
  o he works with central and state governments in the field of education, IT, and business; and
  o he is actively involved in the midday meal program, which feeds poor school kids in many cities across the country.

In spite of all these accomplishments, he exudes humility and courtesy, setting an example for others to follow. He inspires everyone to look for the purpose behind the work first and then decide on how to achieve it.

Mr. Mohan Das Pai

RATAN TATA

The Man behind Tata Swach, the World's Cheapest yet High-Tech Water Purifier

The Tata empire is the largest group in India and is widely diversified when compared to other groups. Its combined revenues or group turnover is around US$100 billion in 2012. The group has a presence in every emerging segment in India and has the following divisions catering to each of the segments: chemicals, consumer products, energy, engineering, information systems and communication, services, steel, and core services.

As per Tata philosophy, the group has to be one among the top three in every segment. Otherwise, the group will move away from that segment and do something else. True to its philosophy, it is either the first or second in each of the segments listed above in India.

What Makes Tata Group Different from Others?

Most businessmen aspire to make money, tonnes of it, and get pleasure from material things that money can buy. When they are more or less done with making money they take up working for a social cause.

But the Tata group, unlike others, has corporate social responsibility (CSR) ingrained in its DNA, and it is done as a part of its business philosophy. Its founder, Jumsetji Nusserwanji Tata, said to his employees, "What comes from society must go back to society many times over", (Jumsetji Nusserwanji Tata, 1890) This statement became

Tata group's corporate mission and went on to become the foundation for doing some of the awe-inspiring philanthropical works in India.

Consider the illustration below to get a feel of what the group is doing and how it is silently doing its part to improve social conditions in India. The following is the list of entities it has founded for CSR initiatives:

- The Tata Institute of Fundamental Research (TIFR)
- The Tata Institute of Social Sciences (TISS)
- Indian Institute of Science (IISc)
- National Center for Performing Arts (NCPA)
- Tata Management and Training Center (TMTC)
- Tata Memorial Hospital (TMH)
- Tata Football Academy (TFA)
- Tata Cricket Academy (TCA)
- Sir Ratan Tata Trust (SRTT)
- JRD Tata Eco Technology Center
- The Energy Resources Institute (TERI)

TIFR is a research institute dedicated to basic research in mathematics and science. The institute is working on cutting-edge research on natural, biological, and theoretical sciences. It is a deemed university and works under the umbrella of the department of atomic energy. It was established in 1945 when Mr. Homi J. Bhaba, who was the father of the Indian atomic program, wrote to J. R. D. Tata, who was the director of the Tata group at the time, to sanction money for establishing a premier institute in India. Money was sanctioned, and the institute was established. Indian Prime Minister Jawaharlal Nehru officially inaugurated it in 1962.

TISS is an institute of social sciences based in Mumbai that offers graduate, postgraduate, and doctorate courses on social sciences with specialization in rural development. The institute has produced some great thinkers like Anu Aga (former chairman of Thermax Ltd.), Purnima Mane (president and CEO of Pathfinder International), Medha Patkar (social activist), and many more. Dorabji Tata established the institute in 1936, as there was a dearth of good institutes that imparted quality education in social sciences.

IISc is a public institution for scientific and technological research and higher education located in Bangalore. It was established in 1908 and became a deemed university in 1958. This institute has been established as a temple of excellence after Swami Vivekananda inspired Jumsetji Tata to establish a scientific institute, as the Institute can form the foundation and the future of India. Interestingly, both Vivekananda and Mr. Tata were sailing on the same ship to Chicago in 1893, while the Swami was on his way to attend the World Parliament of Religions.

NCPA was established in 1966 to preserve classical, traditional, contemporary, visual, and performing arts. Its aim is also to establish, equip, and maintain schools, auditoria, libraries, archives, studios, workshops, and other facilities pertaining to visual and performance arts. The NCPA is the home to Symphony Orchestra of India.

TMTC was conceived and established in1959 primarily to provide management development programs and also create future leaders for the Tata group of companies. In those days, there were no institutes to impart leadership training in India. In this context, the TMTC was established to groom the leaders. The very fact that all the Tata group of companies have become highly successful and are leaders in their segments is because the people who man them have been groomed at the TMTC.

TMH is located in India and was commissioned by the Sir Dorabji Tata trust in 1941, as there were no good hospitals for treatment in India. In 1962, the hospital established a cancer care center for acute lymphoblastic leukemia (ALL). The hospital claims to have a success rate of 98 percent in treatment and cure of ALL.

SRTT is a philanthropic institution established in 1919. The trust was formed in accordance with the will of their group founder, Sir Ratan Tata, who is Jumsetji Tata's son. The main objective of this trust is to become a catalyst for the development of society through funding various developmental agencies. The focus of their grant is toward the organizations that they can partner with for undertaking innovative and sustained initiatives so that a huge difference can be made. They also provide grants for endowments, have separate programs for small grants, and also give grants to individuals for education and medical relief.

The list of nongovernmental organization and government-initiated relief programs that the SRTT is involved in funding is endless. The bulk of its initiatives are toward rural empowerment, community building, and education.

Health-based programs include

- rural health programs;
- mental health programs;
- children with special needs; and
- clinical establishment.

Enhancing civil society and governance:

- youth and civil society
- institution building

Art and culture:

- craft-based livelihood initiatives
- sustaining livelihood through performing arts
- conservation and digitization
- community media and livelihood

Small grants:

- These cater to the needs of small, welfare-oriented organizations and those that need support to implement innovative ideas.

The individual grant program of the trust provides:

- financial help for individuals;
- help for medical contingencies; and
- scholars pursuing higher education in India and assistance for education related overseas travel.

JRD Tata Eco Technology Center was established in 1996 in collaboration with M. S. Swaminathan, an internationally reputed agricultural scientist and his trust, M. S. Swaminathan trust, to encourage sustainable development in agriculture. The JRD center's holistic vision for rural development stretches way beyond farming. That means educating rural people on computers, interaction, and advocacy with the government; educating the poor about the schemes that the state administration has for them; and helping to set up village knowledge centers where the poor can source information on agriculture, health, animal husbandry, horticulture, etc.

TERI was established as a research institute. It is well known and is popular as TERI and was established in 1974. Its research activities are in energy, environment, and sustainable development. According to the civil societies and think tank program (TTCSP) at the International Relations Program, University of Pennsylvania, TERI was ranked twentieth in the list of top global think tanks on environment and ranked sixteenth in the top global think tanks on science and technology.

As per the Tata group's philosophy, they have to be either among the first or second in the market share in each segment they operate in.

Consider this: in the IT segment, Tata Consulting Services (TCS) is Asia's largest in size and revenues; in the chronograph segment, Titan is India's largest watchmaker; in the Indian-branded jewelry segment, Tanishq is India's largest corporate jeweler by market share; so on and so forth. Even if philanthropical work is considered, the institutes started by Tata group top the list of similar ones that are doing world-class work in India. They are either ranked first or second in the survey. For example, TIFR is involved in discovering the neutrino particle (the next biggest project after Higgs-Boson), a project that is going to fructify in 2017. It is considered to be pathbreaking, and if it is successful, it will help physicists know the universe a lot better.

The IISc is rated as an elite institute in India. It is doing cutting-edge research in many areas and offering higher education to people. Many MNCs tie up with the IISc for research-related activities for their future products and services. The IISc was the only institute from India to be ranked by the Academic Ranking of World Universities in 2011 as a premier institute offering quality education. Similarly, other institutes have carved a niche for themselves in the segment they operate in. In spite of their phenomenal success in whatever they are doing, there is hardly any open news about it. Tatas never make much ado about themselves; their work speaks on their behalf. This is an example of how organizations need to wholeheartedly take up Corporate Social Work (CSW) with humility, giving CSW as much importance as their core business interests.

Why Did Tatas Make Swach? How Did They Do It?

Clean drinking water is becoming a rare commodity in India. Around 700 million people living in rural India face serious threats because of the consumption of contaminated water. Around 37.7 million people are affected annually due to waterborne diseases. An estimated 1.5 million children die due to diarrhea alone, and 73 million working days are lost due to consumption of contaminated water each year. The resulting economic losses go up to US$600 million annually. Around 66 million people are at risk due to excess fluoride and 10 million due to excess arsenic in groundwater. Studies done so far have revealed that at any given time, 50 percent of the world's hospital beds are occupied by patients with waterborne diseases.

The situation in urban India is slightly better with civic bodies investing in water treatment plants to cleanse drinking water. The affluent people in cities are able to afford sophisticated water purifiers with reverse osmosis (RO) technology. RO costs a fortune for most of the people, as such purifiers are expensive. In rural areas, though, some people want to buy such purifiers, but because of a shortage of power and irregular flow of water from the tap, they cannot. Also, servicing and the availability of spare parts is a real concern. This being the background, the government has started many schemes to bring clean, potable water to the people. But due to the demography of the country and with the wide spread of habitation along the length and breadth of India, the government's scheme to provide clean, potable water to the masses is not as effective as it should be.

The Tatas, a compassionate and responsible business group, decided to do something so that people get their share of potable water. They had two options. The first was to invest US$1 billion (Rs. 5000 crore) on water treatment plants and another $1 billion in distributing it, which was a prohibitively expensive proposition. The second was to design and develop a cost-effective water purifier and sell it to people either at a subsidized rate through government agencies or sell it at actual rates. In either case, these purifiers should be made affordable to the people who need them.

The Tatas chose the second option and developed a purifier called Sujal in 2004. It was used extensively in the tsunami-affected areas of southern India for providing drinking water to the homeless people.

Sujal used rice husk ash (heating rice husk with pebbles and cement) in the filter. Activated silica and carbon present in the ash reduced the turbidity of the water and absorbed nonpolar impurities. It was later discovered that the purifier didn't have bactericidal properties to kill and remove the bacteria from the water. Also, the filter fell short of the capability to remove a lot of other impurities, such as arsenic, lead, and iron, which brought down the effectiveness of the filter. These filters were withdrawn from the market, only to be introduced again in 2009 with the advanced TSRF technology. Once the ineffectiveness of Sujal was detected, Tata Chemical Ltd., a subsidiary of Tata group and also the promoters of Swach, involved TCS to conceptualize and design TSRF-based filtering technology with input from Tata Chemicals. Titan Industries was involved in designing and producing special assembly presses for mass production.

TSRF Technology

The filter was designed this time with TSRF technology that uses processed rice husk impregnated with nano (10^{-9} or 0.000000001) miniature silver particles for purifying water by killing disease-causing bacteria, germs, and other organisms. TSRF technology also removes other impurities, such as lead, iron, and arsenic, making the water clean and potable. The filter has been extensively tested and verified by government agencies in India, the UK, and the Netherlands to prove the effectiveness of the filter in purifying the water.

The water purifier, Tata Swach, consists of two chambers, one on top of the other. In between is the chamber for the filter cartridge. The untreated water flows from the top to the bottom and gets filtered in the middle chamber. The lower chamber has clean, filtered, potable water. The pathbreaking innovation the Tatas brought was in the elimination of the need for continuous running water from the tap and electricity for the operation of the purifier, both of which are hard to get in rural areas. Tata Swach can purify about nine liters of untreated water at any time, which is found to be suitable for a family of five. The cartridge needs a replacement only after purifying about three thousand liters of water. The purifier will stop working when the cartridge needs a replacement. A bulb mounted on the surface of the purifier will light up, indicating the need for a replacement.

Awards

The hard work of the team has been recognized and rewarded abundantly.

- Product of the Year 2012 award in India
- Won a gold at the Industrial Design Society of America's (IDSA) Design of the Decade award (2011)
- Sniff Award for new product innovation at the Leapvault change leadership awards (2010)
- Asian innovation award in Hong Kong
- ICIS Innovation award, UK

Thus, Ratan Tata finally accomplished what he began in 2004. The group designed an efficient, technically superior, and award-winning, yet very affordable, water purifier for the masses. They are planning to launch the same filter in other emerging countries too. This clearly shows how having a strong purpose behind any work can ultimately bring success.

For details on the Tata group, see: www.tata.in.

For details on the Tata Swach water purifier, see: http://www.tataswach.com.

Tata Swach water filter with TSRF nano technology–based bulb

RATAN TATA

The Man behind Tata Nano, the World's Cheapest, yet Sophisticated Car

India is a continent-sized country with a population of more than one billion (100 crore). It is the world's most culturally diversified country with the culture of people changing every two hundred kilometers. Though it is a developing country, it has some of the world's greatest intellects, affluent people with world-class organizations, and so on. On the other hand, India has the world's highest number of middle—and poor-class people, with the average age being twenty-five. This kind of population can either be a boon or bane to the country, depending on the angle one looks at it from. Generally, younger people have better health and are more optimistic about their future. They are aspirational and ready to work hard when compared to older people.

The business sentiment of any country is based on the optimism of its people. The more optimistic the people are, the better are the economic prospects for that country. This kind of demographic dividend can also be good for those organizations that have products or services to sell. Dr. C. K. Prahlad, the renowned economic professor of Harvard Business School in the United States, talked extensively about the "economy at the bottom of the pyramid." He argues that there is a fortune to be made if companies can cater to these people with suitable products and services that they can afford. The kind of people at the bottom of the pyramid constitutes a majority of the population of any country. This was one of the reasons why the Tatas had strong faith in their low-cost car, Nano, which, if suitably built and priced, would fetch good buyers.

The Nano Story

In 2002, on a rainy day when Ratan Tata, the chairman of Tata group, was traveling in his car, he spotted a family of four on a scooter traveling on the wet road. The entire family was at risk of being killed while riding on the wet, slippery road. This scene made Ratan Tata think of reasons why people rode two-wheelers and braved all the dangers it posed. He realized that families traveled on two-wheelers (scooters, motorbikes, etc.) because they couldn't afford a car. Ratan Tata, being the chairman of India's largest automobile company, decided to do something to make cars affordable for the masses. He wanted to contribute to the safety of families on the road.

There was a wide difference between the cost of a scooter/bike and a car in 2002. The cheapest car was a Maruti 800 cc costing around Rs. 2.5 lakh (US$5,000), much higher than the (approx.) Rs. 50,000 (US$1,000) that a two-wheeler cost. So, after a discussion with the team and internal automotive experts, he found that if the cost of the car was brought down to Rs. 1 lakh, the two-wheeler riders would be willing to upgrade because the difference was not much. These two-wheeler riders would want to use this car for commuting within the city, so the average distance covered by them would be around sixty to eighty kilometers a day. The car should enable them to do so.

Consider this: Indians buy approximately four million two-wheelers every year. Even if 10 percent of those buyers turned to buying Tata's cheap car, it would still be a fascinating number of four hundred thousand. Apart from the Indian market, exporting to emerging markets could be another attractive deal. This was too tempting a proposition and opportunity for anyone in the automotive industry to let go of. These numbers convinced Ratan Tata that the cheapest car in the world had a ready market in India and elsewhere. The question now was: How could they make it that cheap?

In the auto show held in Paris in 2003, Ratan Tata announced to the world his intent to make the world's cheapest car, which would cost approximately Rs. 1 lakh (US$2,000). The car would match all the regulatory requirements with respect to safety, mileage, and performance. This raised everyone's eyebrows, as they were surprised to hear about such an inexpensive car meeting all the regulatory requirements. Some made fun of his proposal, while others ridiculed that it was just wishful thinking on Ratan Tata's part. The world was very pessimistic about his attempt, and there was a reason to be so in 2003. The world economy was growing, and the commodity price was reaching sky-high. All the components, such as the car body and other parts that go into the car, are made up of such commodities. So the world thought that Ratan Tata needed a magic wand that could turn his dream into reality.

Having announced his project, Ratan Tata formed a crack team that could build such an inexpensive car. Girish Wagh, a thirty-two-year-old star engineer, led this team. He was the project manager for this low-cost car project. The car had to be low cost and achieve all the regulatory requirements pertaining to safety, emission, performance, and fuel efficiency. Ratan Tata gave his mandate to the team that the car might be cheap to buy, but it should not be cheap to look at or feel. The team had to work backward, keeping the above objectives in mind. This was unlike all the other automotive manufacturers who build the car first and finally fix the price, considering all the expenses involved in making it, including the profits. This was easier than what Girish was attempting to do.

One morning, Ratan Tata invited some of the world's top component makers and vendors to hear their views on his pet project. The vendor group included Indian companies. They were skeptical about the low-cost car project, as they expressed their inability to make high-quality products at a throwaway price. Ratan Tata impressed upon them the numbers and other market details he had gathered earlier and said that if they could somehow make this work, it would give them tremendous worldwide recognition, as his incredibly low-cost car had become the talk of the town everywhere. Also, it would boost their bottom line like no other car project could, as there was lot of scope in India alone. Over and above, there was an export opportunity for the car to other emerging countries. The prospects looked irresistible for the vendors.

The kind of innovation and technology development that this car project saw was probably not seen by other, previous car projects. This was because the team was trying to achieve the unachievable—that is, to make the world's cheapest car with world-class features. The making of the Nano car by the Tatas is the story of innovation and ingenuity of the people involved.

Consider this: to reduce the weight of the car, new materials were developed for making the components durable, yet weighing much less. Newer ways of making the components were attempted by rejigging and changing the manufacturing process. All this was done with the intention of cutting costs while retaining the quality that the other cars offered.

The Rane group, which makes steering wheels for cars in India, was invited to design and develop the steering wheel for the Nano. The usual automotive steering wheel involves a rack-and-pinion mechanism, and this design wouldn't fit for the Nano because it jacked up the weight. The team at Rane had to redesign their system completely by replacing the steel rod with a hollow steel tube. The steel tube would reduce the weight of the steering wheel and also reduce the cost. To give strength to this design, the entire assembly was designed to have one piece instead of the two found in regular vehicles. This was a major cost reducer, as they saved additional machining and assembly cost. The officials at Rane group claim that they were attempting this for the first time.

Similarly, GKN Driveline, which makes driveshafts for automobiles, was pressed into service to design and develop a driveshaft that suited the Nano. The driveshaft, in short, transfers power from the engine to the wheels. The team spent a lot of time designing and redesigning the prototypes for a driveshaft for the Nano with a rear-wheel drive mechanism. But most of their attempts failed in reducing its weight. The number of prototypes constructed was as high as thirty, yet they were nowhere near achieving what they wanted. They then brought designers from their foreign venture to help the Indian team. Finally, the outcome was the development of lightweight driveshafts with a smaller diameter, which reduced the weight along with the cost.

In the same way, every other vendor has a story to tell as to how he brought innovation and reduced the cost and weight of each component to suit the Nano. Those vendor organizations that had the capability to design were allowed to design the products on their own. The ones that lacked it got help from Tata's own design team. This way, the Tatas gave an opportunity to small and upcoming vendor companies too.

No opportunity to cut cost was spared. Ravi Kant, the former vice chairman and managing director of Tata Motors, was responsible for vendor management and negotiations for the Nano project. Every day, Tata's project team and vendor representatives would meet and discuss every aspect of building the car. This included even the technical issues to design cost-effective products. The team emphasized the simplicity of the production process that was involved in making the components. This was because the simpler the manufacturing process for the production of a component, the more was saved on the cost. Every penny that went into the car was carefully analyzed and seen if it could be saved. This kind of meticulous planning and attention to details resulted in the making of the world's cheapest car—the Nano.

With the successful launch of the Nano, Ratan Tata is now eyeing more such cars that are environment friendly, cheap to buy, and operate using futuristic technologies. Following are the cars.

Tata Mega Pixel: This car has been under development for the last four years. It has an incredibly refined engine that can give mileage of 100 kilometers per liter (kmpl), or approximately 62 miles with one liter of gasoline. It can run for 235.6 miles on one gallon of gasoline. No car has ever attempted to provide that kind of unusual mileage, but Tata's Megapixel is being invented to do that. Ratan Tata says that there are some technologies that are being developed for the first time. They have never been tried in any automobiles before. The car is being designed to have a turning radius as low as 2.8 meters, making it a perfect vehicle to commute in crowded neighborhoods.

Tata air-powered car: There is a race among automakers the world over to build cars that run on alternative fuel, such as battery, hydrogen, or ethanol (a biosubstitute). But what appears promising is the usage of compressed air to fuel the car. Automakers say this technology will take almost three years to perfect. Tata group is in a race with Honda, Toyota, and others to build and bring such cars to the market in the near future. This is a clear indication of how the Tata group operates. It always tries to be ahead of competitors in every segment.

Was There a Clear Purpose behind Ratan's Success in Swach and Nano?

The Tata group companies are known for their project management skills. They execute projects on time and within the budget. There are lots of such cases to prove this point, be it making of Nano and Swach or the acquiring and turning around of MNC companies, such as Anglo-Dutch Steel Company, Corus Steel, the Singapore-based steel company Nat Steel, the acquisition of Britain-based Jaguar and Land Rover (JLR) automobiles, or South Korea's Daewoo's commercial vehicle company. Business magazines are littered with stories of mergers and acquisitions (M&A) going sour and pulling the acquirer and the acquired down into the dumps.

So how is that the Ratan's acquisitions have been profitable so far? In fact, the group's buying the controlling stake in JLR reversed the fortunes of that company, and JLR moved into the profit zone in 2012. It is all because of group's clear strategy.

The acquirer should have a strong reason to buy another company in the first place. Unless there is demonstrable evidence to show how the acquired company (with its innovative products and technology) can value add and shore up the bottom line, the acquirer should stay away from the acquisition. There are many reasons why M&A activities fail. One of the reasons could be the acquirer not doing proper technical and commercial due diligence to know if the acquired company can bring in more profits. Another could be the arrogance about being big and being the acquirer. This could prove to be fatal and devastating for the acquirer.

The acquirer has to instill confidence in the employees and the management of the acquired while merging it. Any fault in the execution could lead to failure. So, the success of merger is dependent on how strong the acquirer aspires to merge the two entities and bring about benefits. This calls for a lot of homework before even placing the first step. The Tatas know what exactly they want for their business. So from the wants, strategy always evolves, and behind the strategy is a strong purpose and burning desire. Building of trust and good relationships with the team of the acquired company is very important, as the M&A activity may invoke some kind of fear of layoffs in their people. This fear in the people may make them not cooperate with the buying team, and the deal may end as a fiasco. The Tata's natural ability to win the minds and hearts of people, along with their mastery of people management and building trust, have taken them toward success in the M&A game so far.

Similarly, their purpose behind inventing Swach and Nano was to help meet the aspirations of the people on the lower rungs of society and also turn it into a profitable business model. Two birds were killed with one shot, as the old adage goes. The making of Nano seemed impossible for everyone, but not for Ratan Tata. Everyone in the industry was skeptical about building such a low-cost car, but for him, there was that undying confidence somewhere deep in his heart that was saying, "Yes, it is possible." This was because all great inventions, discoveries, and explorations appear impossible in the beginning. The people who cracked them faced ridicules from naysayers, critics, and others. If not for their unflinching confidence, burning desire, and sincere commitment, none of the great achievements could have come to the fore.

Ratan had a formidable task to get the buy-in from his own employees and vendors in the first place. He had to convince them that the project was doable before he could break the news to the media. The team had to face challenges from the beginning till the cars were rolled out from Sanand plant in Gujarat state.

Initially, the team was confused as to whether it should scale up a two-wheeler to a four-wheeler with additional safety or strip down a normal car and remove some of the expensive features to make it affordable for US$2,000.The design team initially came with a prototype that just had steel bars instead of doors on both the sides, making it look more like a quadricycle than a car. Plastic sheets were positioned on the sides to drain away rainwater to the ground. This was not what Ratan Tata had in mind. For the Tatas, the largest automobile makers in India and a group known for its prowess in science and technology, this was a sheer embarrassment. So the prototype was rejected outright, and Ratan Tata demanded the car be designed from the ground up.

Similar issues cropped up with the engine too. Initially, the team thought of having a smaller power engine and was unaware of how small it should be. Initial prototypes had a 540 cc engine, but the team felt it was underpowered while testing on the road. As a result, it was rejected. To arrive at the optimum capacity of the engine, the team had to iteratively increase the power of the engine and finally settled for 623 cc. This was found to have sufficient power to carry a family of four on the road. The foot pedal had to be realigned to give legroom to the driver.

Initial issues regarding lack of ideas cropped up because of the team's exposure to traditional ways of designing automobiles. In such people, the mind always hovers and thinks only in conventional ways. Out-of-the-box thinking was not possible. So the more such people there are in the team, the more acute the problem of thinking differently becomes. To break this logjam, young designers with an average age of around twenty-five were infused into the team. Their thinking was fresh and without any bias, and that did the trick.

Finally, the car was built and brought to the Auto Show in Delhi in 2009. It was a breathtaking moment for the country in general, and the crowd gathered in the Auto show premises in particular. When the car was unveiled, everyone was surprised to see the six-foot tall Ratan Tata effortlessly step in and out of the sleek, state-of-the-art, futuristic-looking Nano. This made an immediate impact. The news was instantly beamed across the globe, and the world took note of the arrival of India on the world stage as original designers of an incredibly low-cost car with world-class features.

The story of Nano is not just about innovation but also about the change of mind-set that made the impossible possible. This story also brought into the limelight young, aspirational, world-class designers, who, if trained and groomed properly, could design anything from automobiles to airplanes to defense products to computers.

There is a saying: necessity is the mother of all invention. This was the case with the Tata's invention of Nano and Swach also. There was a need for a low-cost water purifier and a car for the masses in India. Ratan Tata and his team understood this need precisely and found a way to meet it. They delivered what the people wanted and became heroes in the peoples' minds. The purpose behind the making of Nano and Swach was to make these products affordable to the masses at the lower end of the pyramid and turn into a profitable business.

What Are the Other Lessons Organizations Can Learn from the Tatas?

The Tatas are good at building trust with all the stakeholders, be it employees, clients, vendors, shareholders, or the general public. Their products invoke trust and guaranteed quality in the minds of the people. This is a phenomenal achievement and is built over a long period of time by consistently giving quality products to their clients.

When it comes to building employee relationships, they are second to none. To know more about their relationship with their employees, let us consider their steel plant in Jamshedpur, in Jharkhand state of India. The group's founder, Jumsetji Tata, with the intent that his steel plant would represent the future of India, built this steel plant in 1907. This was the biggest steel plant in the whole of Asia and a model plant for the entire world. He was a visionary and envisaged a lot of things for his employees at his steel plant, such as model housing, places of worship, modern schools, and other amenities, including a sports complex, swimming pools, good roads, and clean water. He built a modern town around his steel plant, and the employees felt they were fortunate to live and work there.

The skeptics may argue that this happened more than one hundred years ago, but this cannot continue in this age of intense competition. For the Tatas, the employee's relationship with the management is still as cordial as it used to be when the steel plant was built. The big question that comes to mind is: How do the Tatas do it, while others fumble?

The importance of employee participation has been high for the Tatas from the beginning. They always thought that the key to the employee harmony was to make them stakeholders in what they do. When this happened, the employees took pride in what they were doing and gave 100 percent for the cause. This employee ownership boosted the company's performance and profitability, resulting in increased benefits to the employees. So it was like a win-win cycle. As the employees worked with more and more pride and ownership, the company made more profits and the employees benefited more. The workers' involvement resulted in better plant utilization and better product quality. Other organizations can perhaps learn this from the Tatas for their success in the long term.

Why Should One Care for Employee Welfare?

Employees form the backbone of any company, and it is good for the management to keep them in good stead to achieve the purpose for which a company is formed. Companies utilize employees to churn out raw materials into finished goods using machines. They cannot be made redundant using robots, though in some cases robots have overtaken humans to do repetitive, risky jobs. When the employees succeed, the companies succeed. Employees succeed when they are happy.

The question is: What makes the employees happy? Employees are happy when their welfare is taken care of through their salaries and other benefits. There has been a debate worldwide as to how much is too much regarding employee welfare.

Welfare is roughly defined as the ability of the employee to afford living in a reasonably decent house, educate his kids, and take care of other basic needs of his family.

For the employees to get involved in their work, their minimum welfare should be taken care of by the company. Some companies, under the pretext of a hire-and-fire policy, try to exploit employees as the products they manufacture become commoditized, with the margin relentlessly falling due to competitive pressures. This creates pressure on the company's finances to keep the welfare schemes extended. Though there is no direct solution for this kind of problem, the best way out is to automate using robots or any other means so that repetitive work is not passed on to the employees. This way they can avoid keeping the employees exhausted at work. Companies usually resist investing in automation due to the cost factor; making the employees do that kind of work still works out far cheaper than automation. So they cling on to humans and use them as mechanical tools like robots, which leads to fatigue and frustration. Because the profit margins are wafer-thin, these workers get low pay and have to work hard in double shifts to earn a decent living. This kind of monotonous and hard labor leads to employee burnout and may trigger unrest and strikes in the factories.

The wise thing would be to invest in automation, as such investment fetches good returns in the long run. It is better to keep the number of employees to a bare minimum and utilize them only where their skills are required. The Tatas are good at this; their policies are very much humane in nature. None of their factories or offshoot companies has faced any employee strikes or unrest throughout their life span—that is, for more than one hundred years now. They somehow manage the cost pressures with upgraded products so that the margin remains minimally affected. Their employees' welfare scheme remains as strong as ever, keeping them happy.

Organizations need to manage their businesses well to avoid situations such as the one described above. One tip could be to innovate continuously and strive to be one of the top two companies in their segments. This is the only way to survive the competition. The Tatas, as a philosophy, cannot accept not being one in the top two in every segment they operate in. This philosophy makes them innovate, research, and do whatever is required to retain their top spot. When organizations are ahead of others in their product or service offerings, they naturally command a premium in the market and take pride in being ahead of others. When they are profitable, they can pass on the benefits to their employees, adding to their welfare. This will make employees happy and keep them motivated. The Tatas do it this way.

Another accomplishment of Ratan Tata

Ratan took over as Chairman and CEO of Tata group in 1991 when the group revenue was US$ 50 billion (Rs. 2.5 lakh crore). By the time he retired in 2012, the group revenue had touched the magic figure of US$ 100 billion (Rs. 5 lakh crore). He contributed US$ 50 billion to the group revenues in 20 years span. This is a huge accomplishment by any standards. However this pales in comparison with the aspirations of Cyrus Mistry—current Chairman and CEO of Tata group, who took over from Ratan. Cyrus, who is still in his forties, aims to take the group revenues to US$ 500 billion by 2025 in almost 12 years from now. Whether he will be able to do so or not, only time will tell. But by announcing his big plans upfront, Cyrus is showing-off his long term vision for the group. He is a man with big dreams, and has an uphill task to realize them. Perhaps having a strong desire or a dream is the first step towards success. So, he has taken his first step already and has begun his journey towards making Tata group a US$ 500 billion global conglomerate in 2025.

Awards and Recognitions

The Tata Nano won many prestigious awards. Some of them are:

- Car of the Year, *Business Standard Motoring* (2010)
- Auto Car of the Year, Bloomberg (2010)

- The car bagged the first place in the transportation category given by Edison awards in 2010.
- Global Design Award (2010) This award is annually conferred by the Museum of Architecture and Design, United States, together with the European Center for Architecture and Art Design and Urban Design.

For details on the Tata group, see: http://www.tata.in.

For details on the Tata Nano, see: http://www.tatanano.com/home.htm.

Mr. Ratan Tata with his baby, Nano

CAPTAIN C. P. KRISHNAN NAIR

The Man behind the World's Most Admired Leela Group of Luxury Hotels

In the world of luxury hotels, the Leela group stands out, as it operates a chain of palatial hotels and resorts in Mumbai, Bangalore, Gurgaon, New Delhi, Chennai, Goa, Udaipur, and Kovalam. All are Indian cities. These hotels are known for their exuberant luxury and the world-class service they offer to their customers. In fact, the arrival of the Leela group of hotels brought in a sea change in the Indian hospitality industry with high standards, so much so that others found it difficult to match.

These palatial hotels, with international platinum-level standards, are the result of one man's dream and aspirations to make it big in life. He is Capt. C. P. Krishnan Nair, the founder of the hotel chain, born in 1922 in a remote village in the state of Kerala in southern India.

He was born in a poor family, but his ambitions and aspirations were always big and unmatchable. Even though he was born in a sleepy town, he has been leading a vibrant life. In his early years, he had joined the Indian national army, founded by none other than the revolutionary leader Subhash Chandra Bose, and served there for quite some time. He is patriotic to the core and always wanted to do something for the country. It was this patriotism that later made him join the Indian army after India gained its independence. He served as a captain for some years and quit from the services in 1950 when he married a girl called Leela.

He later joined his father-in-law's handloom mill, which was running under losses. He started helping his father-in-law to market the goods abroad by starting to export business in a small way and later took over the management of the business. He was successful in developing and marketing hand-spun yarn from India, called bleeding Madras in the United States He turned his company into a pioneer in making and exporting quality bleeding Madras fabric, which became very popular worldwide during the 1960s.

During the 1980s, he introduced many fabrics that were hitherto not made in India. One among them was laced garments, which he made at Leela Scottish Laces, a factory in Mumbai. Later these garments were exported too.

During one of his visits to West Germany in 1957 with an Indian handloom delegation, he experienced five-star luxury at Hotel Kempinsky for the first time in his life. He was so overjoyed that a seed of desire was immediately sown in his heart to build a similar hotel in India under Leela's name. So, whenever he traveled abroad to the West, he made sure that he stayed in five-star hotels, experienced the service, and felt pampered. The spark of desire that had ignited in him earlier turned into a burning flame now. This made him decide he had to act on his desire at any cost. Though he started his work in the 1960s, it was only in 1987 that he was able to open his first five-star hotel, Leela Kempinsky, under a license agreement from Kempinsky, Germany. The luxurious hotel was located near Sahar International airport in Mumbai. The Leela Kempinsky in India became the talk of the town and soon became a hangout for the rich and famous.

Captain Nair, a passionate businessman, a wonderful husband, a good father, and a friendly person to work with, achieved success due to his endeavor to pursue excellence in whatever he aspired for. He has shown to others what it means to work hard with a strong purpose and settle for nothing less than perfection in whatever one does. Consider the fact that he was the one who helped the government of India in 1951 to establish the Handloom Development Board so that lots of poor handloom weavers could benefit from it. He influenced the government to agree on imposing one paisa on every meter of mill fabric woven as tax. The result was that Rs. 300 crore (US$60 million) could be collected in the kitty through which much of the mill modernization could be carried out. Over the years, this board became a force to reckon with, as it encouraged the weavers to adopt modernity in their work so they could export and earn money in dollars. This was precisely what happened in the later years.

He achieved excellence in 2001 by becoming the largest individual clothing exporter from India and received the prestigious Golden Globe award from the Department of Textiles in India. This was a big credit for someone who had no clothing experience per se before he got into this business. His hard work and passion for doing things right the first time made this possible. Apart from this, his accomplishment in hotels is worth mentioning. Though he started his career in the hotel industry at the age of sixty-four, his achievements are no less spectacular; in fact, they sometimes far exceed those of ones who started their careers at a very early age. He went on to establish a chain of luxury palatial hotels and resorts throughout India, and each of the properties went on to become an icon, bagging some award or the other.

To measure the kind of aspirations or big dreams he had, one should look at the achievements of his splendidly built five-star deluxe hotel, The Leela Palace, which was built in 2011 in New Delhi for a whopping Rs. 2,000 crore (US$400 million). The hotel went on to be named as one of The Best of the Best Hotels on Earth in 2012 by *Robb Report* in its annual ranking. It is the authority on ranking the most prestigious luxury hotels around the globe. Apparently, The Leela Palace in New Delhi is the only hotel in India to be chosen for this prestigious award for meeting and exceeding the world-class standards set by the *Robb Report* team. This is a tremendous achievement for Captain Nair, and one can imagine how much hard work and pain went behind this kind of recognition.

How Has This Been Achieved?

A childlike enthusiasm, bigger-than-life dreams and aspirations, being ever ready to work hard, and never-say-die attitude made him achieve this.

Making of Leela Palace Hotel, Bangalore

Though every Leela hotel has its own story to tell, the Leela Palace in Bangalore has a unique story to narrate about its making. After the success of Leela Kempinsky in Mumbai and Leela resorts in Goa, Captain Nair embarked on a much more ambitious project this time—that is, the building of the Leela Palace in Bangalore. The land was made available on the airport road by the government, and it was up to Captain Nair to build the kind of hotel that represents rising, young, and aspirational India. It was decided that the hotel would be developed to represent the culture of the Vijayanagar kingdom.

Captain Nair agreed to go ahead with realizing his mega dream, even if it stood to cost him a fortune. It was decided to emulate the architecture of the Palace of Mysore as it is an extension of Vijayanagar art and culture. Work began in the late 1990s, and by 2000 the construction was complete. The Leela Palace of Bangalore matched the splendor of the Mysore Palace in all aspects. Be it sheer size, exquisite artwork on the walls, marble and granite flooring, or the water fountains, it was absolutely awe-inspiring.

The services of this palatial hotel should match its grandeur, and to make it really so, Captain Nair did the unusual by inviting members of the royal families of Mysore, Jodhpur, and Baroda to stay in this hotel for a week, experience the services, and rate them accordingly. They were requested to see if the services matched those they experienced in their respective palaces.

At the end of the week, the royal visitors gave a thumbs-up to the service, congratulating Captain Nair for achieving the feat. It became a norm for the hotel to follow this as a format, and it was repositioned as "*Athithi devo bhava,*" meaning "guest is God." The message was "every guest will be treated like a royal king." That became a hit with the guests.

In 2000, Bangalore was becoming the outsourcing hub of the world with executives making a beeline for the city. Being near the airport and commercial hub made all the difference to Leela Palace in Bangalore. It became an instant hit with the executives and tourists. In 2002, *Conde Nast Traveller*, a hotel-ranking agency, in its annual survey adjudged the Leela Palace in Bangalore as "the best hotel of the world." The news flashed all over the world, making headlines in business magazines, and Captain Nair became a hero. That was how a star was born.

How Did Captain Nair Bring Success in Every Work He Took Up? Was It the Strong Purpose behind His Work that Led Him here?

Having a strong purpose behind one's work brings clarity to it, and it becomes that much easier to work on, as one knows what exactly one wants. Similarly, Captain Nair had a strong purpose behind all his work. Though there are many instances to prove that statement, the making of Leela Palace in Bangalore into a world-class hotel that offers princely services to its distinguished guests stands out. To make this possible, he had his hotel's services endorsed by the royalties of Mysore, Jodhpur, and Baroda with the clear purpose of raising the service standards sky-high. Once this was established, he replicated these service standards across the Leela group of hotels in India, with the honest intention that all his hotels should have the same service standards. This would not have been possible if strong desire and purpose was not present behind his work. A strong purpose is like fuel to the engine that puts the vehicle on the move.

Captain Nair, who is already an octogenarian, feels the need for someone younger to steer his business empire into the twenty-first century. His sons are already in their sixties, and so the captain is betting on his three granddaughters to get into the driver's seat as soon as possible and take control. Being young and in their twenties, they can connect with the new age customers pretty well. Also, they are the heiresses to his empire, so he wants them to be as serious and as efficient as him when it comes to managing the business. For these reasons, he is grooming them with the intent of achieving excellence in business.

- Amruda Nair, the eldest granddaughter, currently holds the designation of head of corporate asset management. Her responsibility is to take the Leela brand global. She would explore this opportunity either through management contracts or through an ownership route. With an international master's degree in hotel management to flaunt, and also her love for finance and numbers, she makes a potent CEO for the Leela group of hotels. To add to her qualifications, she also has a postgraduate diploma in journalism from the London School of Journalism. She is editor-in-chief for *The Leela Magazine*, an in-house lifestyle and luxury magazine.

- Aishwarya Nair, the middle granddaughter, is groomed to head the food and beverage department. Her designation is head of corporate food and beverages, with the responsibility of making Leela group of hotels gear up to provide contemporary and traditional food, based on the customers' demands. Because food is an important component of the hospitality industry, it should be managed by an expert who has the necessary background and education. Apparently, Aishwarya has taken courses in culinary arts management from one of the top schools in the United States and worked extensively in the Mandarin Oriental Hotel in New York in menu building, wine acquisition, and much more.

- Samyukta Nair, the youngest granddaughter, is being groomed to take care of the interiors of the Leela group of hotels and involve in efficient operations of the same. Her designation is head of interior design and operations. She has completed her MBA from Ecole hotelier Lausanne, Switzerland.

These ladies have a long way to go before they can manage the show on their own. Captain Nair and his two sons are grooming these young ladies by showing them the big picture and inspiring them to dream big. Once the seeds of big aspirations are sown successfully in their hearts, they can help bring success.

Awards and Recognitions

There is hardly any award under the sky that Captain Nair hasn't won, and it is easy to list those he hasn't won. Here is the glimpse of awards that have been showered on him as a token of appreciation.

- Lauding him as a doyen hotelier, American Academy of Hospitality Services honored him with a Lifetime Achievement Five-Star Diamond award in 2009.
- For his untiring efforts in conserving the ecology, he bagged global 500 laureate roll of honor by the United Nation Environment Program in 1999 from Emperor Akihito of Japan.
- Padma Bhushan award by the government of India (2010)
- Hotelier of the Century award, International Hotels and Restaurant Association based in Geneva, Switzerland

For details on the Leela group of hotels, see: http://www.theleela.com.

Captain Krishna Nair posing behind his Leela hotel in Mumbai

CAPTAIN G. R. GOPINATH

The Man behind India's First Low-Cost Airline, Deccan Airways

The advent of the twenty-first century and the arrival of the new millennium brought with it new breakthroughs in technologies, concepts, and thinking. The great revolution happened when the cost of accessing the Internet fell, while the speed of connectivity rose to an unbelievable level. Also, newer ways to compress the images while transmitting over the Internet and continuous decrease in the ownership cost of personal computers made people Internet savvy. The Internet suddenly became a mass phenomenon.

Now, people can stay connected over chat services like Yahoo! Messenger and MSN Messenger. They can even see and talk with the other people on a real-time basis through the Skype network. All these, once considered just science fiction, have become a reality in the new millennium.

Another concept that silently evolved was low-cost air travel. Air journeys, which were once considered to be expensive and catered to rich people, suddenly became affordable to the people belonging to middle income groups. The first of such airlines catering to the burgeoning middle income group in India was Deccan Airways, started by Capt. G. R. Gopinath. His success story is an example of how an ordinary person with an extraordinary dream and determination can make it big in life, irrespective of what obstacles he faces on the way.

Capt. Gopinath was born to a poor family in a village of Hassan district in Karnataka state of India. His father was a farmer and a teacher. Capt. Gopinath had a modest beginning, as he did his schooling in a government school in his village. He got into the army after passing his board exam. He served in the army for eight years and participated in the 1971 war that liberated Bangladesh from Pakistan. After his stint in the army, he took up the family profession of farming and got into sericulture. He made a difference in that field by introducing ecologically balanced farming techniques to improve the yield and using organic ingredients as pesticides and fertilizers. His farm became a place of attraction for government agencies and NGOs to visit and learn from him the newest eco-friendly techniques he developed for his sericulture business. The people appreciated it, and by 1996 he became an established sericulturist, winning a reward for his farming techniques.

It was in 1995 that he happened to venture into a helicopter charter business in India. The Indian aviation segment was restricted, as it catered to only a few rich people, and those came from only a handful of Indian cities. The people from the remaining cities were deprived of air services; the captain sensed an opportunity and started this charter business. Business houses and rich people in small cities and towns could charter the entire helicopter for traveling purposes. This venture turned profitable, eventually making others follow his footsteps. It was in 2002, when he was flying to Goa from Bangalore, that the idea to start low-cost, no-frills air services came to him. There was a strong reason behind it.

The aviation segment in India was growing at a snail's pace, though the Indian economy was growing fast. The one reason could be the prohibitive cost of flying for an ordinary Indian in addition to limited connectivity. The captain thought that if these two obstacles were taken care of somehow, he could have another successful venture. He started planning and developed strategies to bring down cost and boost connectivity. By 2003, he launched his maiden venture called Deccan Airways, which was a low-cost, no-frills air service connecting many of the tier-two cities to the metros. That was the story behind India's first low-cost airline.

How Did Captain. Gopinath Reduce the Cost of Air Service?

Before the advent of the Internet, air tickets were sold through a network of travel agents. These travel agents used to take their cut on every ticket they sold to individuals. The tickets used to be of hard format—that is, they were printed out on some kind of expensive, colored wax paper and were distributed physically through a courier. This was an expensive affair for the airlines. Apart from this, airlines used to have sales offices across various cities comprising a sales team, accounting team, and administrative staff to take care of each office. This was in addition to a corporate head office in a metropolitan city. The airlines had decentralized, yet cumbersome operations. This was an expensive proposition too.

In addition to the above, the airlines were offering food and beverages to their passengers in the airlines. To maintain high standards, these food items were sourced from expensive eateries/ restaurants, which added to the cost of each ticket. Studies have shown that the passengers were not necessarily in need of these, certainly not at the expense of the high cost of air travel. Another important factor that added to the high cost of tickets was inefficient ways of handling airline scheduling, as there was no centralized, real-time flight information available at that time. The airlines make money when their planes are flying with a high number of passengers on board. That is, the more the planes are on flight, the more money they make. So, instead of keeping the planes flying as much as possible, they ended up being grounded for long periods of time due to many reasons. Some of this could have been because of improper planning, and that could be due to the nonavailability of real-time data. Internet technology changed all this forever.

Captain Gopinath had to take a hard look at these factors and implement a time-tested, proven strategy to work around these avoidable hurdles, make the airlines affordable to the common man, and still be profitable. The first step he took to fix the money leakage was to do away with the booking and ticket-printing tasks from the travel agents; he created a centralized website, or Internet-based portal. This was designed and made accessible to people in India.

People could now log in to the website, book seats, and even take printouts of the acknowledgment receipt through printers on ordinary paper. In case printing was not possible, they could even input the receipt into their mobile phones or any handheld device and produce it at the time of boarding the plane. This strategy saved a lot of money for Deccan Airways and made travel agents redundant.

Once ticketing was centralized on the Internet, the next step was to have a central operation to plan and execute the scheduling tasks. Deccan Airways had one big office set up in Bangalore equipped with the necessary staff for its Pan-India flight schedule. This made a major difference for the airlines, as Captain Gopinath could pull it off with the least number of people and with one major office. The next thing to fix was the revenue leak due to food and beverages provided to the passengers. All the freebies to the passengers were stopped and, instead, were sold to them. This meant that they would get only a complimentary bottle of water; everything else was available at a price. This plugged the last of the revenue leakage holes.

The remaining task was to negotiate with the aviation ministry for cheaper night parking facilities and loans from banks at lower interest rates. He did that and got fair discounts from them.

With this, he kick-started his low-cost airways and made big waves in aviation history. The media carried major stories about his venture, and business journals talked about how Indian aviation could leapfrog into one of the world's most-happening industries. The world took note of it, and foreign airline makers and financiers made a beeline to India, talking to corporates and encouraging them to start similar ventures in India.

Was There a Clear Purpose behind Captain Gopinath's Effort in Starting Deccan Airways?

The captain knew exactly what the issues were with the aviation industry before he started his low-cost airline venture. The issues were, in fact, clear to everyone, including private airline operators who were operating full-service flights before 2003. However, it was only Captain Gopinath who set about fixing them and formulating workaround plans. This he did with the intention of encashing on the savings that would accrue because of his pathbreaking initiatives.

He worked on his strategy with one purpose in mind—to make air service affordable to the common man from even the tier-two cities. He did whatever was required to be done, and the rest is history. Consider this: during the heyday of full-service flights, a one-way ticket between Bangalore and Delhi cost around Rs. 17,000 (US$340). It was extremely expensive for even rich people to fly often. The captain's venture slashed this to just around Rs. 3,000, marking the beginning of the great Indian air rush.

He even brought the culture of bidding to air ticketing and also that of advance booking at never-before heard of rates to faraway destinations. For example, an air ticket from Bangalore to Delhi could cost even less than Rs. 3,000 (US$60) if booked at least ninety days in advance. His detractors and competitors mocked these attempts and criticized him—till they found him successful. Later, they too followed suit. In 2007, the number of leased airlines managed by the Deccan Airways was forty, and the number of passengers it flew crossed the seven hundred thousand figure, making it India's largest low-cost, no-frills airline. He sold his share to Vijay Mallya of Kingfisher Airlines, as the competitors were breathing down his throat by excelling at the game that he started. The aviation market was being saturated by 2007–8, and the next set of growth could only happen by expanding and connecting to some more tier-two and tier-three cities.

That required Captain Gopinath to invest heavily in buying or leasing more planes, which, in turn, required lots of money, and banks were not that forthcoming to lend. Even government policies were not supportive of his low-cost air business, as taxes on aviation fuel were very high. Considering all these factors, it made sense for him to sell, as he felt the time for consolidation had arrived in the airline industry. Nevertheless, his passion for flying and making a difference in the airline industry made him start yet another new venture, this time in the air cargo segment. He called it Deccan 360.

Captain Gopinath wanted to revolutionize the logistics and distribution business the same the way he did with his airways. He worked on the hub-and-spoke model by locating the hub in Nagpur, which is considered to be the heart of India. He is currently making big strides in his cargo business, and competitors are watching his moves closely, indirectly endorsing his right strategies. His newest venture is a regional airline to connect tier-two and tier-three cities to state capitals. He has started it in Gujarat (a state of India), connecting all the small cities and towns to bigger cities and the state capital, eventually connecting to Mumbai through five twelve-seater aircraft. This story tells that no matter how difficult the path is, one has to work in a field of his choice, something for which he has passion and will strive to be successful.

Awards and Recognitions for Captain Gopinath's Hard Work and His Vision

- In 2007, the French government bestowed on him the award *Chevalier de la legion d'Honneur* (Knight of the Legion of Honor) for his contribution in the field of aviation that brought India and France closer.
- In 2005, he bagged Karnataka Rajyostava award from the Karnataka government.
- He was awarded with Rolex Awards for Enterprise in 1996 by the Rolex watch company for his sericulture business and his new eco-friendly techniques to help the people and the environment.

Captain Gopinath, founder of Deccan Airways Limited

N. R. Narayana Murthy

Founder of Infosys, One of the World's Most Admired IT Companies

N. R. Narayana Murthy—the very name kindles hope, trust, hard work, sincerity, humility, modesty, and great vision. He is the face of new India.

<u>Early Years</u>

N. R. Narayana Murthy had a humble beginning. He was born in Mysore, a city in Karnataka state of India, in a middle-class family and was brought up with a strict code of conduct and virtues in life.

He completed his bachelor of engineering in electrical from Mysore University in 1967 and his master in technology from the Indian Institute of Kanpur in 1969. His early career stints were in IIM Ahmedabad and Patni computer services before he started his own maiden venture, Infosys Technologies, with just Rs. 10,000 (US$200) in 1981. His current net worth alone is US$1.7 billion in 2012. A small seed sown in 1981 went on to become a gigantic tree bearing millions of such seeds. This is his story of success. In fact, all six of the founders who struggled to raise money during the early years of Infosys had become billionaires by 2012.

How Did They Do It? How Was Infosys Different?

Infosys was formed by highly educated youth who were aspirational, yet ready for any sort of struggle to make Infosys, their venture, a success. They were all sure that they would succeed in life but never dreamt that it would be such a grand success. They became the talk of the town in India and the world over. People look at Infosys and admire its impressive buildings and get carried away by talk of the tonnes of money these founders and shareholders have made. What they do not understand is the pain these founders experienced before they could succeed in life. Consider this: when Infosys was started in 1981, India was very different than what it is in 2012. It was at the peak of the Cold War era, and with its socialistic affiliations, India had probably the maximum number of hurdles for private companies. The economy was under the iron grip of the federal government, which was the sole decision maker about who would produce what.

When bureaucracy was at its height, Narayan Murthy and other cofounders started Infosys. During the late 1970s till the mid-1980s, there was a great demand for customized software. Manufacturing systems in the United States and Europe were becoming complex, and IBM mainframes started playing a central role. There was a need for professionals to write software codes to manage the manufacturing operations through these mainframes. That was how the idea of starting a company to do the programming sprouted in the minds of the Infosys founders. On June 2, 1981, Infosys was registered. They wanted to base the company in India and deploy the people in various clients' offices to do programming work. All of the six Infosys founders had a fair amount of computer programming experience prior to starting the venture.

Starting the company was easy compared to running the show. It took nearly a year to get a telephone connection, as the telephone department's priority was to give connections to government employees, bureaucrats, and others, both on duty and retired. Giving a telephone connection to a business was the least of their priorities in those days. The Infosys founders had to run from pillar-to-post to get one single business telephone connection. That too happened after repeated efforts for one year. The telephone line would frequently go dead, as quality of service was quite bad. Infosys did not have a single computer till 1983. India's federal bank, the Reserve Bank of India (RBI), had a strange law that stated if you wanted to import a computer from overseas, then you should deposit two times the value of the computer in the RBI account in Indian currency. To earn that kind of money, someone would have to be deployed overseas. But again, for going abroad, there were a whole lot of hurdles. Foreign currencies, such as US dollars and British pounds, were very scarce; because of that, the government restricted people from carrying these currencies while traveling abroad. So, with all the requests and persuasions, the banks would give negligible amounts of foreign currency, and travelers were encouraged to manage with the paltry amount that they got to carry abroad.

In such a scenario, the Infosys founders used to travel overseas. They managed by staying in some relatives' houses or budget hotels, eating inexpensive food while working, and saving money at the clients' offices. Every penny they saved was routed back to India to import new sets of minicomputers, mainframes, etc. The unity among them and their shared perspective about professional and personal life made them stick together and face challenges with unity. This made a big difference for Infosys.

Another challenge they faced was about communication with their clients abroad. In those days, e-mail was not heard of; messages could be exchanged only though courier or speed post. International calls were prohibitively expensive and were not an everyday mode of communication. So the messages from the clients to Infosys officials or vice versa, and between Infosys offices in India and abroad could reach very late. Because of this time lag, the messages would lose their relevance. As if these problems were not enough, Infosys faced many other issues too—issues relating to liquidity or cash flow, managing the employees' expectations, human resource policies, and so on.

The founders started fixing these problems one after the other as they arose. Many times the founders had to mortgage their possessions when they fell short of liquidity and never let these problems come in their way. This shows their fiery resolve and steadfast belief in themselves and their hard work. They proved to the world that all problems had solutions, provided one looked at the problems with the mind-set of solving them.

Though the company was registered in 1981, it became equipped to fully operate only after it acquired its first minicomputer in 1983. Its first overseas client was Data Basics Corporation from the United States. The order was executed from Bangalore, as the registered office had moved there from Pune that year. When the business grew, they bought mainframes and some more minicomputers for business purposes the following year. In the following years, Infosys struck a deal with Kurt Salmon, an American strategy-consulting firm and made good strides in business. The venture failed by 1989 due to some differences of opinion, and the founders were devastated. They suddenly felt their identity was lost and felt their future was sealed. That was the time when most of the founders thought they must have made a mistake by starting a company and were more or less ready to give up and do something else. If it were not Mr. Murthy's strong resolve to stick to what he believed in, the other founders would have left him and Infosys. Murthy said with courage and conviction, "If you all want to leave, you can. But I am going to stick (*with it*) and make it", (source: www.citehr.com).

He was even ready to steer through the storm all by himself in case the others went away. Buoyed by Murthy's confidence, they stayed with him, and the rest, as they say, is history.

The 1990s saw the phenomenal rise of Infosys under the stewardship of Murthy as its CEO. By 1993, the company it was listed in the BSE. Stalwarts such as Mohandas, Hema, and many others joined the team and took responsible pole positions. They helped Mr. Murthy bring transparency in the operations and executed some of the projects that Indians had never heard of earlier. The agenda of Infosys was the cocreation and sharing of wealth through excellence. So the performance of every employee in Infosys mattered a lot. This called for recognizing the merit and hard work of the employees, which became the yardstick to measure and decide who would share how much of the wealth. This was how Infosys differentiated from others. In other organizations, the connections to the founders mattered a lot when it came to recognition of the performance of their employees. Talented and skilled people who had no connections with any industry founders flocked to Infosys, making it a magnet to attract the best of talents, as scaling up the career ladder is relatively easy there. Infosys's strength grew day by day, and by 2012, its employee strength was more than 150,000, with offices and software development centers in most major cities across the globe.

Achievements of Infosys

Everyone around the world was bowled over by the importance given to ethical values and virtues by the founders of Infosys. Though prior to Infosys, there were many Indian companies operating in India with offices in other countries, the kind of visibility, acceptance, and recognition that Infosys received had not been experienced by any other company. This was because Infosys brought many firsts in India and the world. Consider this: Infosys was the first company to write an HR policy tailor-made to white collar jobs in a software company, taking into consideration all the factors. Other companies later implemented its HR policy by reconfiguring it to suit their requirements.

Infosys was the first company to experiment with the offshore development model, where a majority of the employees were located in India but working on software projects that could be exported via magnetic disc or even transferred through Internet connectivity to its clients' offices. This model became a huge success and was one of the key reasons for the mushrooming of software companies in India. MNC companies later successfully executed this model in other countries too. Infosys was the first company to create an open financial policy to bring transparency in accounting, which was appreciated by chartered accountants and other professionals. It was the first company to boost the confidence of the investing community by enhancing the transparency and disclosure levels.

Infosys was among the first companies to have two accounting standards, one for the Indian investors and GAAP standards for overseas investors. Infosys was the first company to list in NASDAQ in 1999, signaling the arrival of Indians on the world stage. It was also the first company in India to be inducted into the Global Most Admired Knowledge Enterprise (MAKE) Hall of Fame. Infosys was featured among twenty-two stalwarts such as Dell, GE, IBM, Accenture, Microsoft, and Hewlett-Packard (HP). The award was for its keenness in organizational learning and its ability to effectively transform enterprise knowledge into shareholder value. Infosys won this iconic recognition for three consecutive years in 2003, 2004, and 2005.

In another first, Infosys was the first company in India to introduce Employee Stock Option (ESOP) in 2000 to share its success with its employees. ESOP was an incentive for employees' hard work so that they could share wealth like all shareholders do. This certainly induced animal spirits in the employees, making them take on more responsibility and work harder. Their hard work brought more profits, which, in turn, led to higher share value. In addition, in 2008 Infosys constituted the Infosys Prize, a way to recognize and monetarily reward budding scientists, technologists, professors, and others in India for their contribution to engineering and computer sciences, mathematical sciences, life sciences, physical sciences, and so on. This prize is an Indian equivalent of the Nobel Prize. This award has been acclaimed and appreciated by many in India, as it recognizes and rewards the hard work scientists and others put in and encourages them to do more, thus making Infosys a true trailblazer in every field they venture into.

These accomplishments talk about the cultlike image Infosys has built for itself in the world. The list of awards and recognition is certainly endless and difficult to put down here.

Accomplishments of Narayan Murthy

From the beginning, Narayan Murthy has been known for his hard work, vision, patience, and modesty. All these qualities would have been useless if he had no purpose in life. It was this strong purpose that was behind his extraordinary hard work, focus, and great achievements in life. Simply put, purpose is like fuel to a vehicle—fuel that makes people do things that otherwise would have been kept in abeyance. To start Infosys and bring it to the position it is in today, one common thing was needed in the founders: big aspirations.

Narayan Murthy, being the prime mover, a leader among the founders, had plenty of above said skills. He had the attitude of a winner and was not ready to settle for anything less than excellence. Narayan Murthy served as the chairman, founder, and CEO of Infosys Technologies for twenty-one years. Nandan Nilekani succeeded him in 2002. Narayan Murthy is the chairman of the governing body of the International Institute of Information Technology (IIIT) Bangalore and the chairman of the governing body of IIM Ahmedabad. He also serves as a member of advisory boards of several educational and philanthropic institutes, including Cornel University, INSEAD, Ford Foundation, the UN Foundation, and the Indo-British Partnership; he is a trustee for the Infosys Prize and the Rhodes Trust that manages Rhodes scholarships. He is chairman of the governing board of the Public Health Foundation of India; he was a member of Asia Advisory Board for British Telecommunication Plc, and in 2005 he cochaired the World Economic Forum (WEF) in Davos.

Time magazine listed him in the top ten list of global leaders who would influence the future of world technology in its 2004 edition, and in 2005 Murthy was voted as the seventh-most-admired CEO/ chairman in the world in a global study and ranking of CEOs by Bourson-Marsteller, along with Economist Intelligence unit. The list is long and endless.

He was conferred the following awards for his relentless and untiring service to the world of business and humanity:

- Padma Vibhushan by the president of India
- Officer of the Legion of Honor by the Government of France
- Padma Shri by the president of India

- Commander of the Order of the British Empire (CBE) by the UK government
- IEEE Ernst Weber Engineering leadership recognition award by the Institute of Electrical and Electronics engineers

Perhaps the iconic towers of Infosys Technologies in the sprawling IT complexes with their state-of-the-art infrastructure indicate the trials and tribulations that Murthy and other founders went through in building them brick by brick.

Even after all these achievements, Narayan Murthy remains as humble as ever, exhibiting his childlike enthusiasm in whatever he does and setting an example for others.

For details, see: http://www.infosys.com.

Mr. Narayan Murthy, cofounder of Infosys Technology Limited

Babasaheb Neelkanth Kalyani

The Man Who Changed the Face of Indian Engineering Forever, Globally

I t was the mid-1990s, and the government had just opened the gates for foreign investments in India. An enthusiastic middle-aged man, who was managing the then medium-sized company "Bharat Forge" in Pune, set out for an exploratory tour of Europe. While visiting an MNC automobile company, the man introduced himself as an auto part maker in India and expressed his willingness to supply to the auto company. Upon hearing this, the executive of the host company just stopped short of taking hold of his collar to throw him out of his office for making such a ridiculous suggestion. That was the kind of impression the world had about India and Indians those days.

This incident must have hurt Kalyani's pride; it became a trigger for him to do something about it. He devised and executed a plan to raise the quality standards of his products to international levels. Within a span of twelve years, he became the sole supplier of forging parts for the same company in Europe where he had almost been thrown out. He did what he vowed to do soon after the incident. Not only did he make Bharat Forge the second-largest forging maker in the world, but he also changed global perceptions about Indians for the better. Consider this: in 2012 approximately 70 percent of his group's US$2.5 billion revenue came from exports, and he has around 40 percent of the global market share in all the segments he operates in—such is his accomplishment. His international clients are some of the highly reputed, quality-conscious automakers of the world. This is Mr. Babasaheb Neelkanth Kalyani, a businessman par excellence, a visionary, an enthusiastic leader, and a technocrat for the world.

It is due to visionary businessmen like Kalyani that Indian engineering prowess has received global recognition. He has been a true leader with high aspirations and a global mind-set. When most Indian companies were struggling to survive against the onset of MNC companies after the 1991 economic reforms of the government, Kalyani was not only working toward strengthening his base but was also strategizing to go abroad and directly sell his products to foreign buyers. He was a big dreamer and dreamt of making his company on par with his counterparts in Western countries when it came to quality, innovation, and technological adaptation. He did what was required, and in a span of two decades, he turned his humble dream into reality. Consider this: one in two heavy-duty trucks in America runs on axles made by his company in India. He conquered the global markets, showcasing Indian technological strengths. The world admired his Indian-engineered products, as they were equal in quality to Western products but at Chinese prices.

To achieve anything in life, one has to have a strong zeal toward the cause. Sometimes enthusiasm emerges from big aspirations and dreams that people have in their lives, and they tend to pursue these dreams relentlessly. Other times, the zeal or desire emerges as a result of wounded pride due to real or imaginary circumstances. In this case, desire turned into such a burning fire that it may never let the person rest till the objectives are met. The person usually gets into this mode to prove a point to his adversaries. Those who have taken this path would stop once their points are proven. But a few would continue further, maybe to become better than their opponents and even strive to become market leaders in the segments they operate. Kalyani seems to fall into the latter category.

THE POWER OF PURPOSE IN LIFE

A Brief History

Kalyani had humble beginnings in Pune city of Maharashtra state of India. He received his bachelor of engineering from BITS Pilani, India, and Master of Science from Massachusetts Institute of Technology (MIT) in the United States. He later joined his father's small forging unit called Bharat Forge in Pune in 1972. The revenue of the then Bharat Forge was US$1.7 million. He worked his way up like any other worker and rose to become chairman and CEO of the Kalyani group, a conglomerate of world-class companies. He was among the first to understand the importance of bringing a revolution in manufacturing, by transforming it from a muscle power-led to brainpower-led system. He felt that what was applicable in the twentieth century couldn't cater to the requirements of the twenty-first century. So change was inevitable, and those who resisted would perish.

He was convinced of the need to simplify the manufacturing process and introduce mechanization through machines and robots wherever applicable. Redundant manual laborers would be retrenched through a mutually beneficial scheme.

How Did He Make the Impossible Possible?

Mr. Kalyani set out to make Bharat Forge an internationally reputed company with respect to quality and innovation. Initially, no foreign company was keen to establish joint ventures with him for technology transfer, as his company was unheard of and was based out of India. Unless Bharat Forge became a well-established company, foreigners would not tie up with it for technology transfer. To become well established, it needed help from foreign companies. This led to a vicious circle, which Kalyani wanted to break at any cost.

He recruited some of the top auto men from reputed companies abroad, paying top salaries and promising them exciting work opportunities. He took the help of headhunters for this. Once these people were on board, they worked closely by establishing world-class systems and processes to manage production, quality, material, and human resources. Workers with advanced qualifications and work experience were required to handle these processes. So those workers who were in sync with the new requirements were retained, and others were let go.

Kalyani also introduced freshness into management by bringing talented youngsters from the top B-schools and engineering colleges in India. The move charged up the management and resulted in visible changes in the quality of products through innovation and employee motivation. This, in turn, resulted in bagging new orders from MNC car companies, such as Ford, GM, and Hyundai, which had set up their Indian operations by the late 1990s.

Now Bharat Forge was established and could talk on equal terms with foreign component makers.

Kalyani brought in a few executives of those much-hyped foreign companies to show them his factory in India. They were really taken aback when they found Kalyani's factory had more advanced infrastructure than their own. So they were ready to seal the tie-ups. Initially, the agreements were for contract manufacturing, as Indian currency was undervalued and labor was very cheap. Once the buyer and seller relationship grew stronger and after looking at the technical strengths of the Indians, the clients decided to also pass on the design and development works to Bharat Forge. Slowly and steadily, the company became an engineering powerhouse in design and development for reputed global auto clients. The success of Bharat Forge convinced other manufacturers to invest on technology and break away from just labor arbitrage. Kalyani group and other auto component makers collectively made India one of the world's engineering design and manufacturing hubs.

To aggressively cater to international clients, Kalyani opened offices in key auto hubs of the world. He bought companies from across the globe that were financially sick but technologically healthy and could add value to his company's activities back home. By 2012, Bharat Forge became the world's second-largest forging makers with operations spread worldwide and supplying to the who's who of the top automakers of the world.

Next, it was the time to look for businesses in the nonauto domain in order to take some of the risk out of his business. This was required, as whenever there is any downturn in the economy, the automobile business is the first to get the blow. Kalyani diversified into aerospace engineering, wind power technology, power plant engineering, infrastructure, specialty chemicals, and IT, because the knowledge and experience he had gained in component making could now be used in these new areas. These were the areas that were seeing a spectacular growth in India. But this time, he was looking at the complete system rather than merely a portion of it. That meant end-to-end—from concept, design, and engineering to manufacturing and post-sale service. Kalyani started companies servicing in these domains.

To groom his employees, he tied up with Warwick University, BITS-Pilani (India), and IIT Powai (India) for employee education and training purposes. The education program helped existing employees upgrade their knowledge as required to keep up with the technology. Kalyani also recruited graduates, postgraduates, and PhD students from renowned institutes for his mission to bring excellence to all the companies he incubated. As a result, the turnover of the group zoomed to Rs. 12,500 crore (US$2.5 billion).

What began as an attempt to raise the stature of one company to international standards resulted in starting more than ten world-class companies that technologically compete with international players on an equal footing; yet, they all belong to one family—the Kalyani family or the Kalyani group.

Awards and Recognitions

Mr. Kalyani received a lot of recognition and awards for the yeoman service he rendered toward internationalizing the Indian engineering industry. A few of them are:

- Padma Bhushan award from the president of India for his contribution toward trade and industry (2008)

- Recognizing his contribution toward improving business between Sweden and India, the Swedish government conferred him with Commander First Class of the Royal Order of the Polar Star' in 2008.
- Global Economy Prize award, Kiel Institute
- German Businessman of the Year, *Business India* magazine (2006)
- Entrepreneur of the Year for Manufacturing, Ernst & Young India (2005)
- CEO of the Year, *Business Standard* magazine (2004)

For details on Bharat Forge, see: http://www.bharatforge.com.

Mr. Baba Neelkanth Kalyani, chairman of Bharat Forge

PHANEESH MURTHY

The Marketing Genius, the Man behind the Making of India's Tenth-Largest Software Firm, iGATE, in a Remarkable Eight Years

I n December 1992, a man in his late twenties alighted from a plane at Boston's Logan International Airport and moved to a small hotel downtown. Boston was in the middle of a bitter winter, and the entire place looked as if it was whitewashed. That year, Boston saw one of its worst winters in recent history, as it snowed all through the week. It was the first time he had come to a foreign country, and it was an amazing experience for him to see people from different cultures and races. He was a vegan by birth, and there was no vegetarian food available in the town. He lived on bland-tasting pasta and occasionally french fries with a hot chocolate drink. The man's US stint as a marketing manager took off that way.

Before leaving for the United States, he had promised the then CEO of Infosys Technologies, Mr. Narayan Murthy, that he would bring business worth US$1 million in the very first year. He had just one year to prove himself from the day he landed in the United States. This man not only brought Rs. 5 crore (US$1 million) worth of orders within one year but also helped Infosys revenue grow from a mere Rs. 10 crore (US$2 million) to Rs. 3,500 crore (US$700 million) in the next decade. He was instrumental in launching Infosys Technologies' business process outsourcing (BPO) division and brought enormous success to that division.

In fact, during his tenure as a marketing director, there were so many orders flowing into Infosys that the team back in Bangalore had to struggle to make big strategies to fulfill them. Some business magazines called him the "marketing genius," "order machine," and so on. His name is Phaneesh Murthy. The phenomenal success of Infosys Technologies is partly attributed to Phaneesh, as he was heading the client facing team at Infosys Technologies, United States, as a marketing director. Simply put, he was the face of Infosys for all the clients across the globe and was well versed in handling them. He built such a rapport with clients that most of them would come back to Infosys with more orders. Phaneesh attained a cult like status in a short span of one decade. He was single-handedly responsible for bringing the magic of marketing into the IT industry in India. Phaneesh's success as a marketing director attracted talented marketing professionals in droves to the Indian IT industry.

Previously, only technical people would do the marketing for IT companies, which was not effective, because marketing is a different ball game and requires a different skill set. The success of Infosys, driven by a marketing genius like Phaneesh, convinced other companies to hire seasoned marketing professionals to sell their software products and services. This act changed the face of the IT industry forever, resulting in more and more outsourced orders flowing in from foreign clients to Indian companies.

When everything was going great for Phaneesh at Infosys Technologies, a lady staff member lodged a complaint in the federal court complaining he had sexually harassed her. This scandal brought his career at Infosys to a creaking halt, as he had to resign from the company and face the suspicion of wrongdoing. He came back to India and started from scratch all over again. This was an unceremonious fall from grace for a person who was a self-made man and had achieved dizzying heights of success when he was just in his early forties. Though he had pretty impressive credentials, none dared hire him because of the stigma attached to him during his US stint with Infosys Technologies. This is his rags-to-riches story, about how he came up in life after the disastrous incident in the United States. But before that, it is good to know a bit about his personality and his background.

Brief Introduction of Phaneesh

Phaneesh comes from a modest background. His parents taught him good virtues and values. He was very aspirational from his childhood days. He wanted to be a world-renowned doctor and sat for the tests of the world's top five medical schools. He got an admission offer from Harvard Medical School with a scholarship. In those days, teenagers were interested in getting into the medical field used to think of graduating from Indian medical schools and nothing beyond that. But for Phaneesh, being just another run-of-the-mill doctor was not acceptable. So he chose the world's best medical school to become the best doctor. He was not content with small things in life—that reveals his king-size ambitions.

If it were not for his father's advice against studying medicine, Phaneesh would have been a world-class doctor by now. As per his father's advice, he instead studied for his bachelor of technology from IIT-Madras and received his master's degree from IIM-Ahmedabad in 1987. He started his career in the same year. His first company was Sonata Software, a small software outfit where he worked as a marketing manager from 1987 until 1992. In 1992 Infosys Technologies was looking for someone who could front Infosys Technology in the United States and head the marketing department for bringing in orders. Phaneesh decided to jump into the fray.

In the interview with Murthy, Phaneesh promised that he would bring orders worth Rs. 5 crore (US$1 million) in the first year itself, which Murthy felt was too ambitious and difficult to achieve. The revenue of Infosys Technologies was US$2 million in 1992. A US$1 million order meant a straight 50 percent increase in revenues in one year. However, reading Phaneesh's confidence through his body language, Murthy decided to hire him and give him a chance to prove himself. That proved to be the ultimate decision for Murthy and Infosys Technologies. The rest is history. For Phaneesh, it would be his first visit to the United States. He literally had no business contacts in corporate America. It was no simple task for him to bag his first US$1 million worth of American orders, as he was a new kid on the block who was culturally very different from mainstream Americans. Nothing hindered him and his desire to make it big in America.

He had to face many challenges initially, be it in communicating with Murthy in India or transferring the finished work from India to US clients, as there was no e-mail, fax, or voice mail facilities back then. Telephone calls were exorbitantly high, making them not very affordable. Compact disks for storing data were not heard of yet, and there weren't printers of today's caliber. In fact, it was a problem for anyone to be in the IT business in India in the early 1990s.

As if all this was not enough, the socialistic mind-set of the Indian government created a lot of hurdles for business organizations to ensure their sustainability or expand. Importing computers to India was not easy then, and the execution of the orders brought by Phaneesh became a challenge as a result. The teams had to share the computers with others due to their shortage.

In spite of these struggles, the targets were usually met on time, no matter what it took the team to do so. The executives in India kept all the pain and hitches to themselves; it was Phaneesh's responsibility to manage the show and keep the customers happy. He did just that and was highly appreciated by the customers. This was how life went on for the executives at Infosys for years, till the Indian government brought the import barriers down. As a result, computers, servers, and other products were assembled and sold in India. Eventually, the executives improved the processes and learnt the art of executing the orders without flaws.

In spite of all these hurdles, the revenue of Infosys Technologies was steadily surging ahead. With the listing of Infosys shares in the Indian stock exchanges, it became the darling of investors. There was clocklike precision in bagging the orders and executing them, even when there was economic turbulence in the world. Phaneesh's stupendous success was because of his strategic leadership, business acumen, understanding of client's business needs, and ability to turn them (these needs) into orders. He was a natural at building rapport with clients. They were so happy that they kept coming back to Infosys Technologies with more orders.

Infosys' shares reached sky-high, and so did Phaneesh's fame. Many articles were written about him and his way of life, with some even calling him a "marketing genius."

Phaneesh's Life post-Infosys

Soon after he quit Infosys Technologies, Phaneesh started Primentor Consulting Services to provide strategic consulting services. His track record in turning Infosys into a multimillion-dollar company in just ten years had made many people seek his advice for furthering their own businesses. Through Primentor, he offered strategic consulting services—that is, he provided advisory services to those clients who wanted to improve their businesses. He shut Primentor down after a year of its start-up, as the business was not going where he intended it to go. The following year he started Quintant Consulting Services with a concept of ITOPS (integrated technology and operations). It was a business outcome-based model, which means the company shared the financial risk with the clients while implementing IT services. The company built all the processes and frameworks required to offer ITOPS service successfully. This was a good proposition for companies to ignore, and many become his customers.

By the end of 2003, iGate Corporation, which was listed in the United States, acquired Quintant due to the fact that it was being steered by Phaneesh and his team of able people. In addition, the team's deep knowledge in high-end and lucrative business consulting made iGate's founders decide to buy it off, as it would bring in newer business into its fold.

At the time of its acquisition, Quintant had revenues of more than Rs. 75 crore (US$15 million). Phaneesh became the CEO for the combined entity. At the time of acquisition, iGate was running under losses. Phaneesh, with his knack of doing business, plugged those losses, which ran into millions. Within a year, he made the company earn profits. This was Phaneesh's second transformation story. By 2011, the combined entity's revenues grew from Rs. 400

crore (US$80 million) to Rs. 1,500 crore (US$300 million) in a span of eight years. This reaffirmed his thought leadership.

In 2011, with revenues of more than US$300 million, iGate bought the Indian company, Patni Systems, for more than US$700 million. This was the first time in Indian corporate history that a smaller company bought over a company bigger in size and revenues. The combined entity's revenues crossed US$1 billion. Phaneesh justified his action of borrowing money and investing in the buyout. According to him, most big customers award their IT contracts to IT vendors that are big in size; they prefer to do business with companies whose revenues are more than US$1 billion. This is to keep away the not-so-serious, smaller companies from participating in the bidding. With the combined entity's revenue crossing Rs. 5,000 crore (US$1 billion), iGate became India's tenth-largest IT company as of 2012. This showcases Phaneesh's phoenix-like rise to stardom from scratch, making it an interesting rags-to-riches story to study.

How Was the Purpose Linked to His Success in Life?

There was a visible purpose behind all of Phaneesh's actions in life. As soon as he stepped foot on American soil, he decided that he would work hard for the purpose of bagging US$1 million worth of orders. His purpose became his goal for that year. Because he was a big dreamer with king-size aspirations, his fire for excelling in America taught him whatever skills were required in the shortest possible time. So his US$1 million of orders came his way not with much struggle but with relative ease.

His success story teaches everyone that when one's aspiration is to excel in life, one doesn't have to worry about one's survival, as one would naturally perform at above-average levels in life. On the contrary, when one's aspiration is just to do average in life, with no passion for anything, he or she will find life boring and dull and have to struggle for surviving in life every day. It is like firefighting always, leading to anxiety, sleeplessness, and disappointments in life. This is applicable to companies too.

Once Phaneesh started meeting his goals on a regular basis, he was never quite content doing routine work. His higher purpose was not merely to get the orders but to also make Infosys Technologies as respected and as awe-inspiring as IBM, GE, HP, Dell, and Apple. He worked with the team in India to realize his dream of turning Infosys Technologies into a respected transnational company. The result was the transformation of Infosys Technology into a global organization with revenues of more than US$700 million in just ten years. This has been Phaneesh's extraordinary accomplishment. His hard work, professionalism, and passion attracts accolades from many as definitive, because they sparkle in this crowded world.

As a token of appreciation for his accomplishments, Enterprising Asia, a Malaysia-headquartered, nongovernmental organization that promotes entrepreneurship in the Asia-Pacific region, awarded him the Outstanding Entrepreneurship Award in 2011 as a part of encouraging entrepreneurship in the region.

For details on iGate Corporation, see: http://www.igate.com.

Mr. Phaneesh Murthy, CEO and president of IGate Corporation

PUTTIGE RAMADAS

The Revolution behind the Indian Machine Tool Industry through Ace Manufacturing Systems Ltd. (AMSL)

Years	1979, 1986, 1989, 1995, 1998, 2001 and 2004
Exhibition	IMTEX (Indian Machine Tool Exhibition)
Participants	International and Indian Machine Tool companies
Awards	Best product Design and Best product exhibit
Company that bagged the awards	(1) HMT (Hindustan Machine Tools ltd), Bangalore (2) WIDIA (Now Kennametal), SPM division Bangalore (3) (AMSL) Ace Manufacturing Systems Ltd, Bangalore
Man behind these awards	P. Ramdas

IMTEX is India's famous Machine Tool Exhibition, where the who's who of the machine tool industry from across the globe flaunt their technologically advanced, state-of-the-art products. Earlier held once every three years, it is now organized once every two years, and the best overall product bags the much-coveted Best Design and Best Exhibit awards.

In such a competitive environment, companies such as HMT, WIDIA, and AMSL won the above awards for their products several times—all under the leadership of P. Ramadas. This speaks volumes about his ability to create world-class, indigenously designed products in India, giving tough competition to products imported from both the East and the West. To understand the importance of P. Ramadas, someone who is considered as the doyen and thought leader of the machine tool industry, let us briefly understand this industry first.

Evolution of the Engineering Industry

After World War II, most of the countries in the world took to capitalism. This unleashed an unimaginable variety of products and services. The quality of these products and services reached a record high level through technological advancement and sophistication, which, in turn, resulted in even more varieties of products. To gauge this, one has only to look at the automobile industry. What was considered sophisticated and state-of-the-art in the 1950s became obsolete and rudimentary in the 1970s. The cars we see today are far more advanced when compared to those of the 1990s.

For example, Toyota introduced its iconic Corolla in 1967 and called it the first-generation car. It was considered a breakthrough product then, with a technologically advanced engine and improvements in safety and comfort. The people hailed this product, and Corolla became a big hit in the market. In 2011, continuous improvement in auto engineering has brought us Toyota's latest version of the Corolla, which is the eleventh-generation car. This implies that eleven different versions of the Corolla have been brought to market, which means every generation of the Corolla included some refinements and improvements over the previous version. The latest generation Corolla is much more evolved in engine performance, driving comfort, fuel economy, safety, and luxury when compared to its previous generation. In fact, this car with a state-of-the-art instrument console looks more like an airplane than a car. The machine tool industry contributed immensely to Corolla's progression.

What Is the Machine Tool Industry?

Vehicles such as scooters, bikes, cars, trucks, and buses are an assemblage of many precision components/assemblies, including engines, shock absorbers, axles, gear boxes, clutches, axles, seats, air conditioners, and brakes. The machines that produce these components out of metal, plastic, fiber, or any other material are called machine tools. The beauty of a machine tool is that it can also produce a machine tool. That is why it is called the mother of machines. They are also called special purpose machines (SPM). The industry that caters to the making of these sophisticated mother machines is called the machine tool industry. It is also called mother industry, because the modern engineering industry rests upon it. It can even be called the foundation for other industries as well. Thus, the machine tool industry is not limited to the automobile industry alone. It caters to industries pertaining to aerospace, shipbuilding, defense, electronics and communication, consumer goods, and host of other industries.

As the saying goes, to gauge whether a country is developed or developing, one should look no further than its machine tool industry. If it is most advanced, the country is naturally a developed one—such is the effect of the machine tool industry on the economy of any country. Germany, Japan, the United States, Korea, Taiwan, and Western Europe have the most sophisticated machine tool industries. On the contrary, BRIC nations, such as Brazil, Russia, India, and China, are now catching up with the sophistication of machine tool technology, with China as the number one machine tool consumer in the world, and India in the seventh position. It is assumed that India is technologically years behind Germany in this industry.

Evolution of the Machine Tool Industry

The need to develop better products necessitated the transformation of the machine tool industry by attracting talented professionals. In countries such as the United States, Japan, Korea, Taiwan, and those in Western Europe where the machine tool industry has progressed very well, it is their governments that gave the initial push. After realizing the importance of this industry and the link it has on the economy, the governments incentivized it by giving tax breaks and passed polices supporting cutting-edge R&D work. Finance was made available at low interest rates to encourage entrepreneurship. Help was offered to the companies that were into design and development of machine tool technology. This attracted many serious entrepreneurs to this industry. Teaching institutes started offering customized courses for students. As a result, the global machine tool industry evolved and flourished. The collective efforts of industry, academics, and the government made all this possible. In fact, the global size of the machine tool industry in 2012 is more than Rs. 50 lakh crore (US$100 billion), a figure unimaginable a few years ago.

Ramadas' Connection

Ramadas has been linked with this industry for more than forty-two years and is considered to be one of the finest technocrats and entrepreneurs that India has ever produced. He is an industry veteran and, having spent his lifetime in it, he is spearheading innovation in the Indian machine tool industry. The journey of his life, *In Pursuit of Excellence* has been one of the most inspiring stories of the recent times.

Ramadas is one of the promoters and managing directors of one of India's most successful and fastest-growing machine tool companies. He conceived Ace Manufacturing Systems Ltd. (AMSL), an ISO 9001:2008 certified company, in 1994 along with other three promoters. In its two hundred thousand-square-foot facility spread on ten acres (4.049 hectares), AMSL produces more than one thousand CNC (computer numerically controlled) machining centre annually. With revenue of US$58 million (Rs. 2,920 million) in 2011–12, the products are of global quality but offered at Indian prices. This endeavor shows the passion Ramadas has for his profession. His journey of success is studded with the philosophy of beating the best, and Ramadas always tries to surpass the quality targets that customers expect from his products.

The strict adherence of quality-cost-delivery and services (QCDS) has made AMSL products very popular across a spectrum of users, which competitors find difficult to match. Its client list includes most of the big automobile makers in India, their tier-one and tier-two suppliers, and Indian small and medium-sized enterprises. In fact, AMSL is one of the leading producers of machining centers in India and intends to replicate its success globally.

To build automobiles of international standards, high-quality auto components are required. To make high-quality auto components, reputed and quality conscious companies, such as AMSL, which specialize in machine tool production, are required. The very fact that global auto majors, such as Ford, General Motors, Hyundai Motors, Toyota Motors, Volkswagen group, Mercedes Benz, Suzuki, Honda, Mahindra, and Bajaj, export Indian-made automobiles to worldwide customers, speaks for the high level of quality standards that Indian products have achieved. AMSL, under the stewardship of Ramadas, is indirectly helping Indian-made automobiles to scale newer heights.

The kind of precision work that happens at AMSL is mind-blowing. It produces a wide variety of machining centers. The range includes vertical machining centers, horizontal machining centers, drill tap machines, twin spindle machines, moving column series, and die mold machines. The accuracy of all these machines, measured in microns, is very precise. The machines have positioning and repeatability values less than ten and five micron respectively. (For a clearer understanding, a human hair's thickness is around eighty microns.) One can imagine the precision at which the machine operates to deliver unimaginable quality products.

It is humanly very difficult to achieve these accuracies consistently. So a CNC system with its closed loop position control ensures the desired accuracy on parts produced from these machine tools. These high-precision products are required for achieving the new euro norms of automobiles, aerospace, defense, die mold, and space industries.

AMSL's ambition is to make ten thousand CNC machines by 2020, making AMSL and ACE Micromatic group the number one in the top ten machine tool companies in the world, and which AMSL's team is ever enthusiastic to achieve. After reading the above facts, one may get the impression that AMSL surely has a strong technical collaboration with some world-famous machine tool company. The reality is that there is none. There is absolutely no technical collaboration with any foreign organization. The technology is in-house with a proud Made in India brand. So the machines AMSL produces are designed, manufactured, and tested by its very capable team, led by the leadership and guidance of Ramadas. This speaks volumes about his in-depth technical knowledge on the subject and up-to-date awareness of industry trends and dynamics. This is a result of his burning desire to prove to the world that Indians are as talented as others when it comes to capabilities and have the attitude to achieve excellence in most areas of engineering and manufacturing.

Ramadas is also ever ready to help others who seek to succeed, even if they are his own competitors. For example, at the IMTEX exhibition in 1995, 1998, 2001, and 2004, under his leadership, the AMSL team bagged the Best Design and Best Exhibit awards for its products. It managed this impressive feat four times in a row, making history in the Indian machine tool industry. However, Ramadas stopped applying for these awards, thus making way for other young and aspiring entrepreneurs to participate and win. All said and done, recognition in the form of an award from the machine tool user fraternity is always motivating and inspiring to young and upcoming entrepreneurs in the machine tool business. Thus, making way for others, speaks of his magnanimity and selflessness.

Ramadas rose from an ordinary boy next door in the 1950s to become a successful entrepreneur, strategic leader, achiever, visionary, dreamer, motivator, and, above all, a compassionate and excellent human being. His rise, however, was not easy. He believes success is not a matter of desire but a product of determination, dedication, discipline, and inspiring attitude. A lot of hard work, struggle, and perspiration have gone into attaining such fame and success.

His Early Years

Ramadas was born in 1946 in Puttige near Moodbidre, which is one of the many coastal villages in the state of Karnataka in India. His father was a farmer who wanted his son to grow up and become an engineer. In those days, schools were not too common, and Ramadas had to walk miles through hilly terrain to reach school. Under such trying conditions, he finished his schooling, scoring exemplary academic grades. He earned his bachelor of engineering from Karnataka Regional Engineering College (KREC) in Suratkal, another coastal town in Karnataka. He completed his engineering degree with flying colors, scoring top grades. Later, in 1970, he completed his postgraduate in machine tools from the premier IIT-Madras. He scored good grades in the postgraduate course too.

With his postgraduate degree in hand and a fire in his belly to make it big in life, he joined Hindustan Machine Tools (HMT) in Bangalore, a premier machine tool company then, as a machine tool designer. He was one of the members of the team that developed the numerically controlled (NC) lathe in 1972–73. He was the recipient of the first Best Design award given to the best machine tool design of the country for the machine exhibited in the IMTEX exhibition in 1979 for his slant bed CNC lathe.

He led the design team to develop India's first computer numerically controlled (CNC) cylindrical grinding machine. He has also presented many technical papers in journals and national conferences. After putting in thirteen years of service in HMT, he took up the position of design head at Machinery Manufacturer Corporation (MMC) and completed a short stint there before returning to the machine tool hub—that is, Bangalore.

In 1984, Ramadas joined Widia (now Kennametal India) in Bangalore to start and head its Special Purpose Machines (SPM) division without any technical collaboration. It was there that he had the best of exposure in R&D, production, assembly, marketing, servicing, and project implementation, which formed the foundation for his future endeavors. At Widia he designed and developed some high technology and advanced SPMs, such as deep hole drilling machines, creep feed grinding machines, an array of SPMs, six axes tool, and cutter grinders, which were the first of their kind in India. During his leadership, WIDIA SPM division got the Best Exhibit award at the IMTEX exhibition in 1986 and Best Design and Best Exhibit award at the IMTEX exhibition in 1989, thus making WIDIA a leader in manufacturing of SPMs in India, a position that it enjoys even today. After his successful stint at Widia, Ramadas joined Mysore Kirloskar Ltd., the oldest machine tool company in India, as vice president of engineering in 1990. His contribution continued to flow in all facets of machine building activity. In a span of just two years, he upgraded the features of CNC machines and developed new products for the company. In 1992 he joined hands with the promoters of Ace Designers Ltd., the largest producers of CNC turning centers in India, to design and develop CNC machining centers. In 1994 he started AMSL to produce machining centers. This is where his inborn leadership skills unfolded in more ways than one, and the following years became history that few could match.

Accomplishments at AMSL

AMSL had a humble beginning in 1994. It was a time when India had partially liberalized the conservative domestic market by opening up its doors to foreign companies for selling their wares in India. There was anxiety and excitement all around: anxiety for the manufacturers who had never cared to upgrade their products and excitement for the consumers who now had a range of products to choose from for the first time. Indian manufacturers, with their obsolete products, began to feel the heat; a sense of inferiority loomed large as they could not compete with the latest products from foreign firms. There was a strong urge in the Indian producers to upgrade their products quickly with a possible tie-up with any foreign company. Importing machines for making products was still expensive because of high import duties. Also, sourcing the finance was still relatively difficult for them, as the banking sector had not yet opened for new entrants.

This was most visible in the automobile and auto component makers in those days. For component makers, the Indian machine tool sector was not developed enough to make a variety of components for the newer generation of cars, bikes, and scooters, which were launched during that time. At the same time, buying the CNC machines from abroad was difficult and beyond their budgets due to the high duty factor prevailing then. Importing from China was the only possibility, but Chinese products had a low shelf life, and servicing was a bigger problem. Machines imported from Taiwan also faced similar issues. It was during such a situation that AMSL was conceived by a visionary leader like Ramadas.

He was a boon for these Indian component makers. This was because, by 1994, he had established himself as a developer of quality CNC machines and had a good rapport with the industry. He had the necessary knowhow, infrastructure, and enthusiasm to produce international-quality machines at Indian prices. So, even with the prevalent conditions then, he could easily make and sell three CNC machines in the very same year that AMSL started. That was a huge accomplishment for him, because AMSL still lacked the kind of infrastructure that it has today. He managed the show single-handedly. There has been no looking back for him since then. AMSL has experienced a steady growth both in size and stature.

Ramadas is a leader of vision and action. His dream is to hit a target of ten thousand CNC machines in 2020. He has an ambitious plan to achieve this. He intends to buy fifty acres (20.24 hectares) of land on the outskirts of Bangalore and plans for his vendors (from whom AMSL buys components) to co-locate with AMSL, thus intending to have vendors located closely around its premises in its new expansion projects. This strategy will be useful in enhancing the quality of local vendors, as greater control could be exercised due to the proximity, to meet global standards and increased capacity. Ramadas is keen to make this happen, and when he is successful, it will have a huge impact on Indian technical capabilities. The vision is to contain the inflow of imported machines as equivalent indigenous alternatives are made available at an affordable price, thus saving precious foreign exchange for the country. This speaks volumes about his foresight, his self-confidence, and the pride he has for his country. He is known as the man with a mission, so it is very likely that he will succeed in his Mission 2020.

AMSL and the Future

To succeed in the long term, any company has to invest in identifying and grooming capable second-line leaders, and AMSL is no exception to this. Ramadas has already begun grooming the second-level leadership and is confident that they will inculcate all his values and take AMSL to new heights in the future. The next progression in the machine tool industry is robotics and automation, which is being used widely in western countries, and the trend will reach India sooner rather than later. To encash this opportunity and get AMSL into the field of automation, Ramadas' son, Dr. P. Vishwas, who has a doctorate degree from Australia, has been entrusted with the charge of overseeing AMSL's new venture.

Art of Building Relationships with Employees: Ramadas' Way

Ramadas is not only a hard-core technologist but a strategic leader as well. He was in an industry that demanded knowledge-based manufacturing. He realized that the people hired from conventional manufacturing industry might not be of any help to him at AMSL, so he recruited college interns and young engineers with less than five years of experience in order to groom them. It is easy to groom young people, as they are flexible, receptive to ideas, open to out-of-the-box thinking, and ready to work hard. The industry requires knowledge enhancement on a continuous basis. Youngsters are more open to do that. Ramadas offered a professional and stimulating work environment with a decent salary. This strategy worked and made a lot of difference at AMSL. Young and motivated engineers came with new ideas, and their work often involved challenging their own intellects. They took pride when their ideas clicked and were turned into innovative products. Productivity soared and so did the company's output. This was because they enjoyed their work.

Ramadas treats his employees not as workers but as family members. The way a father treats his children equally, he treats all of his people with equal respect and honor. He ensures that all the information pertaining to the company's revenues, output (number of machines delivered), and net profits is open to all. There is complete transparency in his dealings, as he feels that his people are his extended family and also need to know this information. This has brought a sense of ownership in all employees, and they are very proud to be working for AMSL. The feeling of "AMSL is our company" has been etched in their minds. The result is clear: from the day AMSL started in 1994, not a single day has been lost due to employee unrest. That is a big achievement and beyond doubt all the credit goes to Ramadas.

When AMSL moved to its current ten-acre plot, Ramadas built a lavish garden for his employees and made each of them sow a seedling. They have their names tagged to the plants. This, Ramadas says, is a symbol of the legacy they leave behind. This is a unique concept, and people went overboard to make sure their plants were taken care of well and so was their company. This act induced emotional bonding between AMSL and its family members.

The garden, complete with fountains, is a treat to the eyes. The natural melody of water splashing on the ground brings in the feeling of being one with nature. All this, Ramadas says, was required to boost the creativity and bring in rhythm and harmony to his people. This sense of ownership has done magic for AMSL. The employees are ever ready to do whatever is required to meet their target and go even beyond it. This has become a way of life at AMSL.

To bring in harmony, all AMSL members meet every day at 8:17 a.m. sharp in the lounge of the facility and pray for the welfare of everyone. They practice *pranayama* (an Indian rhythmic breathing exercise) for energizing their minds, followed by meditation to give mental peace. If anyone's birthday falls on that day, that person comes to the front of the assembly at the end of the morning session, talks about some weakness (everyone has at least one), and takes a vow to overcome it in a year. A mentor or a coach is attached, and that person is encouraged to give up the weakness in one year. The following year before the next birthday, the person should either give up fully or show some improvements in quitting the weakness. This exercise is a part of character-building task that every AMSL staff has to undergo to become a better human spiritually and materially.

Ramadas has an open corporate office culture with no chambers—not even for the managers, CEO, or himself. This is an attempt to bring his people closer to each other and work without any inhibitions. Ramadas sits as one among them, which makes him easily approachable. All the above activities have made the employee relationship with the management extremely cordial, with everyone respecting each other. Overall, there is tremendous positivity in his company.

People First

While he was addressing a congregation of eminent industrialists, Ramadas said "People-driven corporations will have strategic advantage in the twenty-first century", (He quoted it while addressing entrepreneurs of SME in 2011).

He meant that people are specific to an organization, and its culture is unique. Culture cannot be purchased but has to be nurtured and practiced over the years. It is easy to imitate technology but difficult to copy culture. Highly inspired people will not only be able to adapt to the quickly changing environment and manage competition but also meet the challenges of the present context. Highly inspired people with high aspirations innovate, leverage resources, reset boundaries, diversify around core competence, and build new organizational capabilities to meet the global challenges.

His message was crystal clear: "If one can manage one's people—their beliefs, their emotions, their needs and wants effectively—one can manage the organization and its march toward excellence pretty well,"(He quoted it while addressing entrepreneurs of SME in 2011). So investing in people should become top priority for every proactive organization.

This realization has steadily dawned upon corporate circles the world over. A lot of money and energy is being drained in brainstorming, to know how to build an organizational culture that instills a sense of ownership in the employees. Some have seen partial success, and others are struggling without any clues. AMSL is a classic case that can be studied for the lessons on building a culture of ownership in the employees.

It is proven that corporate earnings and employee motivation are connected. Employee motivation can come only with a sense of pride in what they are doing and a sense of ownership in the organization they work for. The key is to make employees feel proud of their company. It is not easy, as it takes long years of patience and hard work to achieve it. As a result of such steps, Ramadas is now reaping the fruits of his past efforts.

Advice to Aspiring Entrepreneurs

Being a successful entrepreneur himself, Ramadas recommends the following to budding entrepreneurs for the development of an excellent organizational culture.

Set high aspirations in the minds of people. Identify the key goals of an organization and start to communicate them to the people as often as possible. This enables organizations to establish a stronger foundation for change and set more achievable, and often higher and more ambitious, goals than they otherwise could achieve. The organization that misreads its people squanders its time and resources.

Change the mind-set of people. This is very critical to the company. Bringing harmony within the various groups of the organizational structure is very important. Most often, the veterans who strongly identify with their roles show the indifference in the organization. The budding entrepreneur should not discriminate between individuals, whether staff or management.

Working on a flat management system and considering everyone as a family member is important. The educational qualification can be considered only at the entry level; subsequently, an equal opportunity should be provided for everyone to excel.

The way people think and feel about their work and conduct themselves in the work place depends on the following.

- leadership alignment and role modeling
- clear direction and compelling purpose spelt out every day
- discipline, collaboration, accountability, and purpose demonstrated by the leader
- focus on the continuous improvement of people in every walk of life
- enhancing effectiveness of individual skills

The lean leaders and their expected habits. Employees don't change if their managers don't. Lean leaders act as role models for their mind and behavior. They should instill the same in their team.

- **A focus on operating processes.** Senior managers should use visible activities to demonstrate the importance of processes and making standardization a habit.
- **Root-cause analysis of the problem.** Managers should fight the instinct to provide immediate solutions to problems, using them instead as teaching and learning opportunities.
- **Clear performance expectations.** A transparent performance dialogue should take place at all levels of management.
- **Sense of purpose.** Connections between day-to-day work and compelling, long-term aspirations should become tangible throughout the company.

- **Working people.** Managers should recognize and demonstrate that frontline working people are a source of customer value. These personnel need to be empowered to make important decisions.

Encourage longer working hours. To anticipate the moves of the competitors, one has to understand how their strategist and decision makers think. Companies need people who are inspired to work longer hours at the workplace to make top management decisions a reality with short execution time.

Upgrade internal talent during downturn instead of head count. Downturn normally places a company's talent strategies at risk. Deteriorating performance forces increasingly aggressive head-count reductions. It is easy to lose valuable contributors inadvertently, as well as damage morale and the company's external reputation among potential employees. On the contrary, one has to use this period to train and develop personnel. Also use the downturn period to create facilities to improve efficiency at the workplace. The positive way of looking at this is by emphasizing the talent in cost-cutting efforts, strengthening the value proposition of the current employees, and positioning the organization strongly for growth when economic conditions improve.

Inspire people to use their hands, minds, and souls. Like the face is the index of the mind, employees are the index of the organization. The core strength of the organization lies in its people. Their work culture; their dedication in every walk of life, open mind, flexibility, physical and mental health, confidence, burning desire, and urge to excel; and their emotional quotient to handle all adversities are all vital to an organization. Gone are the days when people used to work only with their hands. People should be inspired to work with their hands, brains, and hearts for the best results. The present era demands that employees feel that the company belongs to them. The leader of the company takes the role of the father of the family. Strengthening the emotion, spiritual intelligence, and knowledge quotient of the people who work for the common goal of the organization, which is invariably customer delight, should be the priority.

Organizations should create an environment of home at the workplace. Employees are to be treated as family members in letter and spirit. They should feel that they belong to the family and are its integral members. The feeling of oneness inspires everyone to deliver his best at all the times. The management plays an important role in also demonstrating the same thing at all times and sets high moral standards for others to follow with clarity.

Finally, success leads to happiness. Everyone strives to be happy. A famous line from a French psychotherapist, Emile Coue, states: "Every day, in every way, I am becoming better and better", (He quoted it while addressing entrepreneurs of SME in 2011). He is remembered for his formula for change through positive autosuggestion. If an organization can bring in a positive mind-set in its family members, then nothing can stop its journey toward success.

Ramadas implemented the above principles at AMSL and built a very good work culture. He quotes that his family is three hundred members big, as he considers his employees as part of his family. These three hundred, in turn, support another seven hundred directly, resulting in one thousand happy people. The happy life of the one thousand people gives Ramadas the inspiration to do further good for some more people. According to the theory of Karma, one will get back multifold whatever one gives, either good or bad. Ramadas gives love and care to his employees, and they give back love, respect, and admiration through dedication at work with a sense of ownership. He truly displays immense care and concern for his employees from the bottom of his heart without expecting anything in return except their efforts to become excellent human beings and professionals, making this kind of person very rare.

He and his harmonious family at AMSL have made it to the list of fastest growing machine tool companies in India, and they are proud of it. This is the secret mantra of the success of AMSL.

Corporate Social Responsibility (CSR)

The media nowadays is riddled with news about corporate greed from all over the world, indicating how companies often operate with a selfish motive to make money at any cost. On the contrary, Ramadas voluntarily does CSR work. Through AMSL, he provides on–the-job, employment-oriented training to poor youth. He sponsors education of poor children and supports the development of his suppliers. AMSL sponsors many sports and educational events and restores places of worship that are in a debilitated condition to give peace of mind to needy people.

He also sees to the upkeep of roads and streetlight facilities around AMSL.

Was There a Clear and Visible Purpose behind All His Work?

If we examine the life and accomplishments of Ramadas, the following come to the fore:

- dedication to his work
- hard work and perseverance
- passion for his work
- clear purpose behind what he is doing
- discipline in life
- strategic thinking
- never-give-up attitude
- meticulous planning

Without a clear purpose, Ramadas could not have progressed on his work. Every piece of work he undertook—be it designing newer machines, starting AMSL, or creating an environment that induces a sense of ownership in the minds of his employees—had a very clear set of objectives. His advice to people is to not let success go to one's head or take failure to one's heart.

By being a successful engineer-cum-entrepreneur, he exceeded his father's dream. Every father would wish for a son like him. It is indeed an amazing accomplishment for a person with such a humble beginning. Ramadas is humility personified in spite of his towering achievements. He is indeed a true inspiration for generations to come. His message to the next generation is powerful, yet simple: never give up in life, come what may.

For details on AMSL, see: http://www.amsl.in.

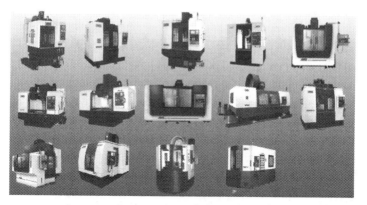

An array of machines that AMSL manufactures

P. Ramdas, managing director of AMSL, in his state-of-the-art factory

Sprawling campus of AMSL in Bangalore.

WOMEN POWER: ANU AGA AND MEHER PUDUMJEE

The Duo That Transformed Thermax India Limited from a Small Indian Company into a Global Conglomerate

The year was 1998; Anu Aga was at the helm of affairs of Pune city-based Thermax Limited, which had listed in the BSE two years earlier. She had taken over the responsibility of leading the company after the sudden demise of her husband, a Harvard-educated professional named Rohington Aga, in 1996. The company's performance was not as per the shareholders' expectations, and the management had put the blame on the prevailing economic recession. It was a letter from an anonymous shareholder addressed to Anu that brought the necessary impetus required to make Thermax what it is today. The numbers tell the story better. Consider this: the revenue of Thermax was Rs. 500 crore (US$100 million) in 1998, and it shot up to Rs. 6,000 crore (US$1.2 billion) in 2012.

So, What Did the Letter Contain That Moved Anu So Emotionally?

The letter contained the frustrations of that anonymous shareholder who blamed the management for not showing interest in increasing the company's share value. He alleged that the management had already made enough moola for themselves;

hence, they lacked the drive. This harsh letter made Anu think about her very role in managing the company's affairs. She engaged Boston Consulting Group (BCG), seeking their advice in 2001. Their assessment was that the company should identify its core and noncore business first and then move away from noncore businesses next. The removal of noncore businesses, the BCG team claimed, could bring sharp, laser-like focus in the areas that defined Thermax's strength. They also advised that professionals should manage the show and Anu could take up a nonexecutive position, such as a chairperson. She did exactly that; thus, the transformation began.

When her husband, a smart business tycoon expired, Anu was managing human resource at Thermax. She was a happy-go-lucky lady, with lots of social activities outside Thermax and did not have any clue how to run an organization. From such a modest beginning, she went on to become one of the top ten businesswomen leaders in India in a short span of five years. She won many awards and recognitions along the way. Under her leadership, Thermax moved into the fast lane of growth, reversing all the shareholders' concerns and bringing a smile to their faces.

This story is about how this happened.

Brief History of Thermax

Thermax Limited was started in 1966 by the late A. S. Bhathena, Anu Aga's father, to harness steam from small boilers built for hospitals. He collaborated with a Belgian company called Wanson. He represented them in India with a manufacturing plant in Mumbai (erstwhile Bombay), a metropolitan city in the western Indian state of Maharashtra. The company's name was changed to Thermax Limited in 1980. Having heat exchange as its core strength, Thermax expanded to relative areas like heaters and chillers and made good profits. The company's revenues reached Rs. 500 crore (US$100 million) by the turn of the last century, and it was when Anu's husband, Rohington Aga—the then CEO and Chairman of Thermax, died of heart attack.

Thermax under Anu's Chairmanship

When Anu moved to the chairperson's role in 1996 after the death of her husband, overseeing professionals was not easy for her, as men were not keen to work under a lady boss. So Thermax saw many CEOs come and go till 2007, when M. S. Unni Krishnan took up that role and stayed with Thermax (as of 2012). So Anu was in the driver's seat with two hats—one of a CEO and the other of a chairperson most of the time.

Thermax was making losses because of aggressive expansion and unrelated diversification into areas that were not in sync with what it was known for. The noncore business areas, such as domestic paints, bottled drinking water, transmitters, electronic components, software, lease and financing divisions, and a few similar ones were not adding much to the share value. These divisions were not yielding much profit yet were demanding lots of focus and attention from the management. Anu took the hard decision to sever them from the main business, either by arbitrarily shutting them or selling them to others.

It required lots of guts, because it involved money, people, and business risks. It was not easy for her, as she had to keep the impact of her actions on the business to the bare minimum. While she was busy with the restructuring exercise, she lost her mother-in-law; in the same year, her twenty-five-year-old son, Kurush, died in a road accident. One can only imagine the grief and emotional distress she was experiencing on a personal front. In spite of this, she was making good progress in the work she had taken up. At last, a woman of such sagacity had achieved what she had begun—making Thermax leaner and meaner by shedding the unnecessary flab.

With a lot hard work, she found out the true identity of her company. The identity was: "A provider of global solutions in environmental and energy engineering",(Mission statement of Thermax, www.thermaxindia.com). Once the true identity was known, the real unleashing of Thermax's potential began, followed by a no-holds-barred growth. Anu now started collaborating with foreign companies with the latest technologies in the areas mentioned above. She acquired the UK-based firm M. E. Engineering Ltd., a provider of design and project management solutions in energy engineering. This act deepened Thermax's service offerings. Later she opened a branch, Thermax Inc. U.S.A., to act as a front end for North and South America and to bring business. Thermax started taking larger environmental and energy-related engineering projects to build and execute them for its clients.

When Anu took over the helm of Thermax, there was no culture of innovation. This was a horrendous situation to be in for any company, as the very survival of companies depended on the productivity and innovation of their employees. Anu not only kick-started the culture of innovation but also made it take the center stage there. Soon, there was innovation in their service and product offerings. It took Anu till 2004 to cleanse Thermax off noncore divisions and bring a performance—and merit-oriented culture in the organization. This set a strong foundation for Thermax so that the next phase of focused growth could come from the solid base set by Anu. Revenues reached Rs. 850 crore (US$170 million) in 2004. Later, Anu decided to take the back seat when her daughter, Meher Pudumjee, was showing the signs of a leader, like her. She hung up her boots and let Meher take over the responsibility of leading Thermax and work toward furthering its business. Anu became busy with her social work, as she was heading a host of NGOs in India.

Anu is a multifaceted woman and is known for the social work that she has undertaken. She has a master's degree in social sciences from the Tata Institute of Social Sciences and a bachelor's degree in economics from St. Xavier College, Mumbai. The thinking at that time, in India, was that women would just get a degree, marry, and settle down in life, taking care of kids and husbands. But Anu went ahead and completed her postgraduate course, which was considered revolutionary. Such is her personality: not to follow another's path but rather create her own.

She is a board member of Akanksha, an organization for the welfare of children. She is on the board of Commonwealth Human Rights Commission. She has taken up the role of vice president of Jnana Prabodhini, an NGO related to women's welfare. She is also a board member of many other social organizations dedicated to the development and upliftment of society. She is a renowned speaker of corporate governance, human rights, and women's empowerment with strong conviction and initiatives. She has been nominated as an Indian Rajya Sabha member in 2012. That means she is a member of parliament (MP) and continues to remain as one of the directors in an executive category at Thermax.

Thermax under the Leadership of Meher Pudumjee

Meher Pudumjee, Anu's daughter, is a chemical engineer from Imperial College of Science and Technology in London. She was living there with her husband, Pheroze Pudumjee, and taking care of Thermax's UK division. She was handling the treasury and the working capital management at the UK center.

When Anu resigned from the position of chairperson, asking Meher to take over her role, Meher was very nervous about it. This was because of the many expectations from analysts and shareholders. Any small misstep might mean a big hit on profits. Moreover, under her parents' leadership, the shareholders were happy, as they gained a lot from appreciation in share value. So it was natural for her to feel anxious, doubting if she could match her parents' performance at Thermax. In a freewheeling interview, Meher quoted that it was her mother's encouraging statement—"An apple tree cannot give oranges, so, you are what you are and do what you feel is right, do not ape us", (Economic times, October 5, 2012). Anu's this encouragement gave her a lot of courage and made her blossom into one of India's most successful businesswomen.

It was when Meher took over at Thermax that the company saw a phenomenal rise in revenues. The stature of the company changed from a medium-sized one to a global environmental and powerful engineering giant with operations in many countries. Meher could attract talented professionals, as they aspired to work for Thermax. A stint at Thermax made a lot of difference for their careers and to their resumes.

Brief Description of Renewable Energy

Globally, there has been increased awareness about the maladies of excessive usage of natural resources, such as petroleum and coal. Petroleum is used to power our transportation vehicles, and coal is used to produce the electric power to energize everything. Excessive mining for coal and mineral oil and their subsequent burning is spoiling the ecology beyond repair. A lot of pollution leading to ecological degradation and climate changes is the results of overexploiting the natural resources. Governments and corporations are trying to reduce their dependence on such resources, tapping instead into freely available, yet nonpolluting resources, such as wind and sunlight to produce electricity. Research has been happening at a frenetic pace to bring down the cost, inducing vibrancy in that segment, as the demand and supply was very huge. This caused a race among corporations to tap the opportunity arising out of this Holy Grail of alternative energy—that is, wind and solar power.

Solar Power Panels

Under Meher's leadership, Thermax started manufacturing solar-based thermal panels that could offer heating solutions up to 250 degrees Centigrade. That means, without burning any fuel and only using the heat from sunlight, its panels could generate steam from water, which could be used to drive the turbines to produce electricity. The process resulted in absolutely no pollution at all. Similarly, the company has solar photovoltaic panels that can generate electricity directly from sunlight and energize all domestic and industrial equipments without polluting the environment. This was a runaway success for the company.

Thermal Boilers

Thermax got into the manufacturing of supercritical boilers under license from the US-based Babcock and Wilcox Ltd. in 2011. The supercritical boilers are used to generate electricity at high efficiency. India had lacked this technology earlier; hence, help was taken from foreign players. Meher chose to get into this supercritical business because India was opening up its power-producing business to private players, and a lot of power-producing companies began sourcing cost-effective components such as boilers. This made good business sense.

Meher also got a wide variety of boilers manufactured for varied requirements in India and abroad. Thermax also got into manufacturing of different kinds of heaters that use many types of fuels (both solid and liquid) for heating purposes. It has heaters that use solid waste (industrial and domestic) as fuel. At one of the MNC coffee-making plants, Thermax used the left over coffee kernels, shells, and other waste as fuel to burn and produce steam out of water. Using this steam, electricity was produced driving a turbine. This way, Thermax proved that it has expertise in producing wealth out of waste. Industrial effluent and sewage water have been big problems for every city, and governments have recently woken up to the importance of treating this wastewater. Thermax has the necessary products and technology to treat wastewater and recycled industrial waste. It also has products to treat river water to make it potable.

Under Meher's leadership, Thermax became a global company providing integrated and innovative solutions in heating, cooling, captive power (small power plant catering to the requirement of a manufacturing plant), water and waste management, air pollution, and chemicals. Meher aimed for perfection in whatever she was doing and later took the standards up to global levels. By 2012, she had taken the footprints of Thermax to twenty-one countries, making it one of the few Indian MNCs to do that.

A woman known for her practical and down-to-earth approach, Meher became an effective interface between her company and the outside world. With her at the helm, the team at Thermax learnt the fine art of winning contracts. This resulted in lots of orders flowing from Indian and overseas clients, pushing up the revenues sky-high. When she took over from her mother in 2004, revenues were just Rs. 890 crore (US$170 million); in 2012 it reached the figure of Rs. 6,000 crore (US$1.2 billion).

What an accomplishment for a woman who once was nervous about taking over responsibility from her legendary mother. With all these achievements, Meher remains as humble and modest as ever.

Awards and Recognitions for Anu and Meher

Anu Aga:

The former chairperson of Thermax Limited who was responsible for turning around Thermax, she was considered for the following awards:

- Awarded Padma Shri by the Government of India (2010)
- Financial Express, Electrolux, Lifetime Achievement award
- One of the twenty-five most powerful women in the business world
- One of the forty richest Indians by net worth, according to *Forbes* magazine

Meher Pudumjee:

- Meher is the chairperson of Teach for India.
- She is on the board of directors in Akanksha Foundation and Thermax Social Initiatives Foundation.
- She was the first woman chairperson for Confederation of Indian Industries (CII), Western India branch.
- *Business Standard*, CEO of the Year (2009)
- Under her leadership, Thermax was listed in Asia's Top 200 Under-Billion Dollar Companies (2007)

- Meher was listed in the Top 30 Achievers in India, *India Today* magazine.

- Financial Express Woman in Business Young Achiever award (2006)

- She was the only invitee to attend and speak at the Asian businesswoman's conference in Osaka, Japan in 2006.

How Did Strong Purpose, Hard Work, and Passion Bring a Turnaround in Thermax's Fortune?

When Anu took over from her husband, her responsibility was to turn around Thermax and rebuild the investors' confidence. Her purpose of work was to do just that.

The action of engaging business consultants, BCG, was the beginning of that turnaround work. Later, success of every work led her to her final goal, step-by-step, and she ultimately achieved what she intended to in a span of five years. Though she faced enormous problems in her personal life, she managed and continued with her work as prudently as ever. This could be because of her passion in what she was doing. Similarly, Meher took over the resurgent Thermax and took its growth to a higher level. First, she worked with the purpose of strengthening the core areas of her company. Then she worked toward making it adhere to stringent corporate ethics, earning goodwill from the investor community and analysts. Later, she strategized and worked toward globalizing Thermax. This has resulted in Thermax's presence in twenty-one countries, making its revenue cross over Rs. 5,000 crore (US$1 billion).

The moral of this story is that whenever one works with purpose, passion, and perseverance, it is natural for success to come. This has been brilliantly demonstrated to the world by this mother-and-daughter duo.

Mrs. Anu Aga, director, and Mrs. Meher Pudumjee, chairperson,
of Thermax Limited

CONCLUSION

After reading all these success stories, one question that comes to mind is: How much success has come from the passion and inborn abilities of these people? The answer to the question is: all. To understand a bit more, let us look at the following example.

Though Rajiv Bajaj and Anand Mahindra are from the automobile industry, their working styles are different; hence, their success stories are different. Read on.

Rajiv is a core bike enthusiast and has an automobile engineering background. He is hands-on when it comes to designing bikes and is very up-to-date with technological trends. He has a natural flair for automobile engineering and was actively involved earlier in the designing of Pulsar. Though he is a businessman now, deep inside he is a bike technologist. One can safely say that technology is his core skill, and the other skills required to do business are added on or borrowed ones. He put his natural skill to work and achieved phenomenal success. His bike, Pulsar, eventually became the world's most profitable bike in a span of one decade.

In contrast, Anand is a businessman at heart. He may not be involved hands-on in designing or engineering any of his automobiles, but he is a strategist and knows how and with whom to get the job done. This he has demonstrated many times, but it was more visible during the turning around of Satyam Computers Limited (SCL). For those who are not aware of the problems SCL has faced, its founder, Ramalinga Raju, used shareholders' money for personal gains and used accounting gimmicks to show profits on the ledger. In reality, the company was facing losses. Anand, with the intention of buying SCL, deployed a team of expert accountants to scrutinize its accounts.

He did this with prior permission from bankers and the government. After rigorous hard work and huge efforts by his teams (accounting, IT, and HR) for more than two years, the problems at SCL were fixed, and it was turned around.

Anand brought SCL under his flagship company, Mahindra Rise, and made it a part of the Mahindra group. This entity is called Mahindra Satyam now and is a profitable IT venture. He did all this without getting involved directly in any of the tasks mentioned above. But he got it done through people so naturally that it is sometimes hard to believe that he was the main man behind SCL's turnaround story. He never seems to be stressed, tense, or worried, even when handling crucially responsible jobs. Anand has always looked calm, composed, and joyful. If it were not for his natural ability, he would have had many stress-related health problems, such as cardiac arrest, diabetes, or high blood pressure, while leading a US$11.5 billion revenue company. But he is fit and looks healthy with a big smile on his face. How does he do it? The answer is that he is a natural strategist and has the ability to identify and put the right people at work and lead them from the front. He is a born leader.

Ratan Tata, another gentleman from the Tata business empire, demonstrated similar skills. He was responsible for a group whose revenues crossed US$100 billion till he retired in 2012. He was a globe-trotting businessman, attending business conferences and meeting with clients across the globe. He was ultimately accountable to the performances of all Tata group companies. It was a nerve-wracking job by any standard, which could have easily wrecked his health. However he looked as composed, calm and cheerful as ever. How did he manage to do it? – It was that he identified and deployed right persons for the jobs, and stayed detached from the business, yet had an iron grip on it through his deputies. This was his natural style of leading his team and managing the business. He was very successful in all of his endeavors. His style of business was natural and in-built for him; it was not something that he got by attending external leadership courses. He used his god given natural skill effectively to bring excellence in his life.

One could see similar natural skills in Jack Welch, former CEO of GE. Though he received his Bachelor of Science degree in chemistry, he was known for his leadership abilities for turning around GE and boosting its net worth 4,000 percent since he took over as its CEO. He too had the natural ability to identify and deploy the right kind of persons on the job and got the work done. He was a brilliant strategist like Ratan and Anand and a core businessman from his heart. It was his natural skill, which he used for bringing in success.

If one analyzes the life of Dr. Shetty, who is pioneering the low-cost, quality health-care model in India, one point that comes to the forefront is that he has a natural affinity for helping people. He is never tired of helping patients and has a lot of patience. He has a deep interest in his medical profession and is a hardcore cardiac surgeon. He is so hands-on in his job that he is always seen in an operation apron, even in odd hours, in a calm and cool state of mind. Unless one has passion for one's work within, one cannot work tirelessly and still enjoy it like Dr. Shetty. In his case, treating patients, consoling them, and boosting their confidence seem to be natural for him, so he enjoys it. All other business skills required to run his state-of-the-art hospital empire have been acquired from outside. Dr. Shetty is a doctor and a cardiac surgeon from deep within, in contrast to Anand and Ratan Tata, who are core businessmen from the heart.

Many more examples can be given showing how the natural skills in people make all the difference in their lives. Similarly, everyone knows Sir Alfred Hitchcock, the brilliant film director and producer. He was in a class of his own. He was famous for his excellence in making suspense and psychological thrillers, movies which have set standards for other directors to follow. When Hitchcock started his work, he had nothing to compare and learn from. He had only himself and his work to compare. In spite of this, he excelled at what he was doing. He knew how to get that fear instilled in the minds of the audience naturally and used that skill to make thriller movies, which brought him honor and glory. He made a very big mark indeed as a star film director and producer in Hollywood.

On the contrary, Sir Charlie Chaplin, a comic actor of the silent era of movies, was known for his humor and his ability to make people laugh. He could do it to the audience even during the grim years of World War I and II. His depicting himself as Hitler was outrageously hilarious in the movie *The Great Dictator* and was absolutely incomparable. He won many awards for his accomplishments throughout his life as an actor. On closer observation, one can understand that his sense of humor was a natural, God-given skill. Though he did direct and produce movies, he was praised for his comic acting more than for his other work. Charlie Chaplin used this skill to bring great success to himself.

Everyone knows Rowan Atkinson, the British comic actor who is popular for his movies *Mr. Bean, Mr. Bean's Holiday,* and *Johnny English,* among others. He is a talented actor. However, his natural talent is in making the audience break into peels of laughter—he has a knack for that. He does it with such finesse that his sense of humor is very original and widely appreciated. So, analyzing his life, one will get to understand that he has passion for acting and has a natural ability to play comic roles. He has used this talent to bring excellence in his life.

Steven Spielberg is a famous film director and producer, yet was a school dropout. He brought in newer ways of directing and producing movies to Hollywood. He produced famous blockbuster movies, such as *Jaws, E.T., Raiders of the Lost Ark, Jurassic Park,* and *Saving Private Ryan,* that went on to become money-spinners for Hollywood producers. The skill and the passion for his creative work are God-given and are inborn in him. He has used them to make a difference in his career and carved an identity for himself as a legendary film director and producer. His net worth is nearly US$3.5 billion. He has got a lot of recognition and awards for his work.

James Cameron is another legendary filmmaker, a director, a deep-sea explorer, and a visual artist. He is considered to be a genius in making movies. He is highly respected in Hollywood, and students at filmmaking institutes study his movies as part of the curriculum. His die-hard passion in all the areas mentioned above and the natural skill to produce world-class movies, such as *Titanic, Avatar,* and *True*

Lies, has earned him countless recognitions and awards one would only envy. He too used his inborn skills to bring immense success and glory for himself.

Joanne Kathleen Rowling, or J. K. Rowling, is famous for writing the children's fantasy book series *Harry Potter*, which has brought enormous wealth to her, making her walk into the billionaire club in a short span of a decade. She is Britain's thirteenth-wealthiest woman, even wealthier than the queen, in 2012. The art of writing such sensational and nail-biting children's books has to come from within. During her preglory days, she went through a very bad patch in her personal life. This made her very determined in life, and she struggled to create an identity for herself, which resulted in her blockbuster book. With the publishing of her books, she became famous as an author of children's literature in the fiction genre. In fact, no author has probably seen the kind of success that J. K. Rowling has seen with her books. Her chartbuster *Harry Potter* books have sold millions of copies around the globe, breaking all the earlier records. She is now a celebrity author. Like any other successful person, she used her passion and her innate writing skill to bring excellence in her life.

Steven Paul Jobs or Steve Jobs, a college dropout, an entrepreneur, an innovator, and a creator of the Apple line of products, ex-CEO of Apple Inc., has been an icon of innovation. If Bill Gates was credited for bringing computing technology from factories, offices, and research houses to an individual level, Steve Jobs was credited with making a boring personal computer (PC) at home very exciting and most desired. He made a difference that way. Though he was a CEO of Apple Inc., he was known more as a technologist, inventor, and innovator. He had the natural skill and passion to think ahead of others when it came to technology and had a knack for looking at things in a different way, unlike others. He was known for his out-of-the-box thinking. That was how he could bring pathbreaking innovation to even routinely used products and make them interesting to own. People swore by him and tried to follow in his footsteps to innovate, such was his influence on people. He too used his passion and inherent skills to strike it rich and bring excellence in his life.

Michael Joseph Jackson (MJ), or simply Michael Jackson, an American artist, an entertainer, and a businessman, made big headlines in the entertainment industry. The *Guinness Book of World Records* considers him as the mass entertainer of all time and the King of Pop. He had an inborn knack to spell magic in the minds of the audience while singing and was always seen working with passion. His album *Thriller* became a huge hit in 1983 and was a watershed moment in music history. It was his original creativity, and he was at his best. Like others, he used his passion and his inborn skills to create an identity for himself in the world of music, thus raising the bar so high that others find it difficult to reach.

Mohandas Karamchand Gandhi (M. K. Gandhi), also known as Mahatma Gandhi, was a preeminent leader of Indian nationalism in British-ruled India. His style of freedom struggle was unique—it involved peaceful, nonviolent civil disobedience. This he termed *satyagraha*. It attracted millions of people to the movement and made the life very difficult for British in India. Mahatma Gandhi's this peaceful non-cooperation movement finally led the British to transfer power to Indians and leave, which was hailed across the globe. Though Mahatma Gandhi was a lawyer, his patriotism and the passion for freeing India was overwhelming. This made him work for the freedom movement as a full-time affair. The *satyagraha* mode of protest was totally of his own making and not a borrowed one. His integrity, compassion for people, reputation for being patriotic, and use of peaceful means to achieve his goals made people across the board call him Mahatma, meaning the Great. He used his ardent love to free India and his inborn skills to mobilize people for the revolution and achieve his purpose.

Orville Wright and Wilbur Wright, the famous Wright brothers of nineteenth-century America, were the inventors of the modern airplane. They studied till high school, yet they built the flying machine that was seemingly impossible. It was their boundless enthusiasm to fly like a bird and their strong belief in themselves that brought out the best in them. Their strong love for flying made them build innumerable models and keep trying till they perfected it. The skills to build the flying machines came from within, and in 1909 they built a faultless machine after a struggle of more than a decade. Their powerful interest in flying and their inborn skills to develop an impeccable flying machine brought them excellence in life.

Walter (Elias) Disney, or Walt Disney, a world-renowned animator, entertainer, motion picture director and producer, cofounder of Walt Disney Studios, and the creator of Disneyland in America, was born in the early twentieth century. He had no formal education in film production or animation, yet he turned out to be one of the world's greatest animators and film producers. He had a knack for entertaining kids through themes based on cartoons that he created. This became a huge hit and later laid the foundation for building the famous theme park, Disneyland, in California. Walt Disney had within him all the ingredients required for making it big in the entertainment industry. He used his powerful love for cartoons and inherent skills to write stories and make animated movies to bring super-duper success to himself.

All these examples highlight one point. If a person has excelled in life in whatever area, be it music, astronomy, philosophy, research, creative arts, or cookery, then invariably that person will use his or her inborn skills, knowingly or unknowingly, in the profession. Such is the influence of this skill in one's success. In fact, one has to choose one's career after a proper evaluation of oneself to see what comes spontaneously to that person. This even includes choosing roles in an organization. Whichever role makes use of one's instinctive skills or abilities, that role needs to be chosen. That is when success comes and that person will be able to make a strong self-identity in the organization. This is followed by name, fame, and money.

So, what is the one key take away from this book? – It is that we have to know ourselves better to excel in life.

Though some may find it difficult to digest this fact, proper introspection can reveal that each one of us is good at one thing at least. And it is this skill that can bring success to us. Hence it is very important to know our inborn skills first, and the purpose of our lives can be built on them. The moment we have strong purpose in our lives, inner joy will set in, and, we will start leading our lives passionately. This inner bliss will lead to good health, which in turn can bring great wealth to us.

When that happens, every moment of our lives will turn out to be a celebration.

So let us celebrate our precious life this way.